M000014639

MISSOURI

DAILY DEVOTIONS FOR DIE-HARD FANS

TIGERS

MISSOURI

Daily Devotions for Die-Hard Fans: Missouri Tigers
© 2014 Ed McMinn
Extra Point Publishers; P.O. Box 871; Perry GA 31069

All rights reserved, including the right to reproduce this book or
portions thereof in any form whatsoever.
Manufactured in the United States of America.

Unless otherwise noted, scripture quotations are taken from the *Holy
Bible, New International Version*. Copyright © 1973, 1978, 1984, by the
International Bible Society. Used by permission of Zondervan.
All rights reserved.

Cover design by John Powell and Slynn McMinn
Interior design by Slynn McMinn

Every effort has been made to identify copyright
holders. Any omissions are unintentional. Extra Point
Publishers should be notified in writing immediately
for full acknowledgement in future editions.

Daily Devotions for Die-Hard Fans

ACC

Clemson Tigers
Duke Blue Devils
FSU Seminoles
Georgia Tech Yellow Jackets
North Carolina Tar Heels
NC State Wolfpack
Virginia Cavaliers
Virginia Tech Hokies

BIG 10

Michigan Wolverines
Ohio State Buckeyes
Penn State Nittany Lions

BIG 12

Baylor Bears
Oklahoma Sooners
Oklahoma State Cowboys
TCU Horned Frogs
Texas Longhorns
Texas Tech Red Raiders

SEC

Alabama Crimson Tide
Arkansas Razorbacks
Auburn Tigers
More Auburn Tigers
Florida Gators
Georgia Bulldogs
More Georgia Bulldogs
Kentucky Wildcats
LSU Tigers
Mississippi State Bulldogs
Missouri Tigers
Ole Miss Rebels
South Carolina Gamecocks
More South Carolina Gamecocks
Texas A&M Aggies
Tennessee Volunteers

NASCAR

MISSOURI

DAILY DEVOTIONS FOR DIE-HARD FANS

TIGERS

IN THE BEGINNING

Read Genesis 1, 2:1-3.

"God saw all that he had made, and it was very good" (v. 1:31).

When they saw their first football, they were flabbergasted; they hadn't known it wasn't round. They were the students who began football at Missouri.

Apparently intrigued by this newfangled sport showing up on college campuses across the country, a group of MU students in 1890 ordered a football through the mail. As Bob Broeg put it, when the boys "went down to the railroad station to pick it up, they were startled to find out that the darned thing blew up crooked."

Austin L. McRae, an assistant professor of physics, suggested the students begin a football team, and they liked the idea. He was promptly elected the first coach. Burton Thompson, the first-ever fullback, recalled, however, that getting enough students to make up a team was a real chore.

Those pioneers "had no training table, no gymnasium, no baths or showers, but a lot of desire." They even had to raise the money for uniforms.

They warmed up with a 22-6 win over a team of students and then officially began football at the University of Missouri on Thanksgiving Day, Nov. 27. Eleven players, a couple of hundred students, and the cadet band rode the train to St. Louis for a game against Washington University. It wasn't pretty; the more experienced Bears drubbed the boys from Columbia 28-0 and even stole their black-and-gold knitted caps as souvenirs.

They returned to the campus "as battered and bruised a lot of men as ever left a football field." Their manhood was promptly challenged by a team of engineers from the school who boasted they should have been sent to St. Louis instead. The varsity gained some measure of respect when it slaughtered the big talkers 90-0.

The first season of MU football had ended.

Beginnings are important, but what we make of them is even more important. Consider, for example, how far the Missouri football program has come since that first season. Every morning, you get a gift from God: a new beginning. God hands to you as an expression of divine love a new day full of promise and the chance to right the wrongs in your life. You can use the day to pay a debt, start a new relationship, replace a burned-out light bulb, tell your family you love them, chase a dream, solve a nagging problem . . . or not.

God simply provides the gift. How you use it is up to you. People often talk wistfully about starting over or making a new beginning. God gives you the chance with the dawning of every new day. You have the chance today to make things right — and that includes your relationship with God.

Many of the student body preferred to stand on the sidelines and hurl derisive comments at our efforts, which they considered huge comedy.
— Burton Thompson on the first-ever MU football team

**Every day is not just a dawn; it is
a precious chance to start over or begin anew.**

TIME FOR A CHANGE

Read Romans 6:1-14.

"Just as Christ was raised from the dead through the glory of the Father, we too may live a new life" (v. 4).

After a couple of campaigns that didn't meet the standards of excellence Gary Pinkel had established, he made some changes. The result was the legendary championship season of 2013.

Pinkel was the architect of a resurrection that "lift[ed] a previously dead program" to three great seasons of 12-2 in 2007, 10-4 in '08, and 10-3 in '10. But then came an 8-5 season in 2011 that "started some chirping among Mizzou fans about whether 11 years of Gary Pinkel were enough. The chirping turned into howling in 2012" when the Tigers landed in the SEC with a thud and a 5-7 season.

"Everyone wanted to change everything. Fire every coach, so on," Pinkel said. But the head Tiger took a careful look at the 2012 season and saw an injury-ravaged "tough year" that didn't call for wholesale changes. "We lost half our offensive line, our starting quarterback," Pinkel observed. "I believe in our program and what we're doing." Thus, he wasn't interested in a massive overhaul of everything he had built in Columbia over the years.

He did make some changes, however. The offensive coordinator left and co-offensive line coach Josh Henson was promoted. The splits of the offensive line were tightened, an acknowledgement that SEC defensive linemen were too fast and too athletic to give them extra room on their way to the Missouri backfield.

Some of Pinkel's more interesting changes were aimed at reducing injuries. For the first time in his career, he did away with two-a-day preseason practices. He also eliminated a period at daily practice in which the starters went against each other with full contact, full speed. And he scaled back August conditioning.

The changes helped to produce a healthier team and a landmark season. The Tigers were the champions of the SEC East, won twelve games, and beat Oklahoma State in the Cotton Bowl.

Anyone who asserts no change is needed in his or her life just isn't paying attention. Every life has doubt, worry, fear, failure, frustration, unfulfilled dreams, and unsuccessful relationships in some combination. The memory and consequences of our past often haunt and trouble us.

Simply recognizing the need for change in our lives, though, doesn't mean the changes that will bring about hope, joy, peace, and fulfillment will occur. We need some power greater than ourselves or we wouldn't be where we are.

So where can we turn to? Where lies the hope for a changed life? It lies in an encounter with the Lord of all Hope: Jesus Christ. For a life turned over to Jesus, change is inevitable. With Jesus in charge, the old self with its painful and destructive ways of thinking, feeling, loving, and living is transformed.

A changed life is always only a talk with Jesus away.

We didn't come in and start changing everything.
— Gary Pinkel on not making wholesale changes after the '12 season

In Jesus lie the hope and the power
that can change lives.

IN GOD'S OWN TIME

Read James 5:7-12.

"Be patient, then, brothers, until the Lord's coming" (v. 7).

Mizzou's coach was patient and Illinois' wasn't. Thus did the Tigers land one of the greatest volleyball players in school history.

Molly Kreklow grew up in the volleyball heaven of Delano, Minn., where the sport often received more support than the high school football and basketball teams. She was so good that she became a local celebrity.

When the colleges came calling, the logical choice was MU. Molly's uncle, Wayne Kreklow, was the coach in Columbia, and her aunt, Susan, was Mizzou's director of volleyball. But her uncle decided not to pressure her, to back off and let her make her own decision. "I wanted to make sure that if [she played for Missouri], she would have made the decision whether or not I'm the uncle," Wayne said. His patience paid off big time.

"I was really set on going to Illinois," Molly said. However, she "wanted to make my choice on my own time and when I was ready for it." The Illinois coaches grew impatient, though, and began to pressure her for an answer. Kreklow said they told her, "We need you to commit. Otherwise we're going to get somebody else." Miffed, she told them to do just that.

Kreklow arrived at Missouri in 2010 and went to work exceeding the sky-high expectations that met her. As the team's setter

— the equivalent of a quarterback — she led Missouri volleyball to unprecedented success: NCAA tournament berths in 2010 and 2011. Then came the incredible 2013 season when the Tigers won the SEC championship. They were 35-0 when Purdue felled them in the second round of the NCAA Tournament.

Kreklow led the nation in assists and was a first-team All-America and the SEC Player of the Year. *Volleyball America* called her "the top setter to take the court this season."

For Missouri, patience really paid off.

Have you ever left a restaurant because the service was too slow? Complained at your doctor's office about how long you had to wait? Or fumed because a traffic light refused to change?

It isn't just the machinations of the world with which we're impatient; we want God to move at our pace, not his. For instance, how often have you prayed and expected — indeed, demanded — an immediate answer from God? And aren't Christians the world over impatient for the glorious day when Jesus will return and set everything right? We're in a hurry but God obviously isn't.

As rare as it seems to be, patience is included among the likes of gentleness, humility, kindness, and compassion as attributes of a Christian. God expects us to be patient. He knows what he's doing, he is in control, and his will shall be done. On his schedule, not ours.

They pressured me a little bit [to commit]. I said, 'OK, that's fine. I don't want to go there anymore.'
— Molly Kreklow on Illinois' impatience

God moves in his own time, so often we must wait for him to act, remaining faithful and patient.

GOOD TIMES

Read Psalm 30.

"You turned my wailing into dancing; you removed my sackcloth and clothed me with joy" (v. 11).

The first hint that Missouri football was about to experience some good times came on an afternoon when the starting quarterback was in a cast and apparently couldn't run the ball.

On Dec. 18, 1957, Dan Devine was named the university's head football coach. His first team was 4-3 on Nov. 8 when Colorado came to town, but the Tigers had not beaten a team with a winning record. That mediocrity seemed to continue as the Buffs led 9-0 at halftime. "The MU offense was anemic," in large part because junior quarterback Phil Snowden was on the sideline after breaking some bones two weeks before against Iowa State. He had been released from the hospital only the Monday before the game. Trainer Fred Wappel formed a plastic cast that fit Snowden's back and allowed him to walk. He suited up for the game and jogged a little bit, but didn't expect to play.

At halftime, though, Devine asked him if he were willing to give the cast a try. The head coach warned Snowden, "Make sure you don't run the ball. Do the minimal amount and see if we can generate some offense."

Did they ever! As Snowden recalled it, the Tigers scored five times in 11 minutes. He passed for two TDs and, ignoring his coach's pointed instructions, ran for two more. "Devine just was shaking his head on the sidelines," Snowden said.

Mizzou wound up blasting Colorado 33-9, and some very good times were indeed just around the corner. Devine would lead the program for thirteen seasons with a 93-37-7 record that included a pair of Big Eight championships. In the 1960s, Missouri was the only program in the country never to lose more than three games in a season and had the nation's eighth-best winning percentage.

And MU fans got their first glimpse of what was coming on a day when a quarterback with broken bones bailed the team out.

Here's a basic but distressing fact about the good times in our lives: They don't last. We may laugh in the sunshine today, but we do so while we symbolically glance over a shoulder. The Tigers pull off the upset today and then turn around and lose later. We know that sometime – maybe tomorrow – we will cry in the rain as the good times suddenly come crashing down around us.

Awareness of the certainty that good times don't endure often drives many of us to lose our lives and our souls in a lifestyle devoted to the frenetic pursuit of "fun." This is nothing more, though, than a frantic, pitiable, and doomed effort to outrun the bad times lurking around the corner.

The good times will come and go. Only when we quit chasing the good times and instead seek the good life through Jesus Christ do we discover an eternity in which the good times will never end. Only then will we be forever joyous.

A golden period was about to begin [in Columbia].
— Writer Steve Richardson in the wake of the 1958 football season

Let the good times roll — forever and ever
for the followers of Jesus Christ.

YOU NEVER KNOW

Read Acts 26:1-20.

*"'[I]n all Judea, and to the Gentiles also, I preached that
they should repent and turn to God" (v. 20).*

You just never know about college football. If you don't believe
that, consider what happened on Oct. 21, 1972.

That afternoon, second-year Missouri head coach Al Onofrio
took his football team to South Bend to be cannon fodder for Notre
Dame. The Irish were 4-0 and ranked seventh in the nation. The
Tigers were 2-3 and were coming off a 62-0 pasting by Nebraska
the week before. The bookies knew exactly what kind of game it
was going to be; they rated Notre Dame a four-to-five touchdown
favorite and quit taking bets on it.

Sure enough, just as everybody knew would happen, Missouri
had only three possessions in the first half — but it wasn't because
of anything the Notre Dame defense did. The Tigers controlled
both the tempo and the football and converted all three of those
possessions into touchdowns.

On its first possession, Mizzou drove 46 yards on twelve running plays, converting three fourth downs. Junior halfback Leroy
Moss took a fourth-and-two pitch from quarterback John Cherry
and went 16 yards for the score that capped the drive.

Notre Dame recovered to tie the score, and everyone just knew
the rout was on. Nope. Missouri led 21-14 at halftime and then
rolled to a 30-14 lead in the fourth quarter before winning 30-26.

TIGERS

Playing in a steady rain, the Tigers didn't commit a turnover and forced the Irish into four mistakes. "The ball was just as wet on both sides," groused Irish coach Ara Parseghian, who, like everyone else, had had no idea what was coming his way.

You never know what you can do until — like Missouri vs. Notre Dame — you want to bad enough or until – like Paul – you have to because God insists. Serving in the military, maybe even in combat. Standing by a friend while everyone else unjustly excoriates her. Undergoing agonizing medical treatment and managing to smile. You never know what life will demand of you.

It's that way too in your relationship with God. As Paul, the most persistent persecutor of the first-century Christians, dis-covered, you never know what God will ask of you. You can know that God expects you to be faithful; thus, you must be willing to trust him even when he calls you to tasks that appear daunting and beyond your abilities.

You can respond faithfully and confidently to whatever God it is calls you to do for him. That's because even though you never know what lies ahead, you can know with absolutely certainty that God will lead you and will provide what you need. As it was with the Israelites, God will never lead you into the wilderness and then leave you there.

Even the heavens wept as Missouri pulled off the biggest upset of the 1972 college football season.
— Indianapolis Star *on the Tigers' win over Notre Dame in 1972*

**You never know what God will ask you to do,
but you always know he will provide
everything you need to do it.**

TROUBLED TIMES

Read Nahum 1:1-8.

"The Lord is good, a refuge in times of trouble. He cares for those who trust in him" (v. 8).

You would think that if a team shuts down the Big 12's Offensive Player of the Year in a bowl game, Missouri would be in real trouble. Nah.

The Tiger passing game and the Arkansas running game received most of the hype before the 2008 Cotton Bowl. And why not? The Hogs featured the dynamic duo of Darren McFadden and Felix Jones. MU countered with junior quarterback Chase Daniel, the league's offensive player of the year who finished fourth in the voting for the Heisman Trophy. As a senior, Daniel would become Mizzou's total offense leader, passing Brad Smith.

Arkansas' defense had one purpose: to stop Daniel. It did. The Razorbacks frequently dropped as many as nine players into pass coverage; as a result, Daniel threw for a season-low 136 yards and no touchdowns. If the Hogs succeeded in their defensive game plan, then logically the Tigers must have been in trouble.

It didn't turn out that way. An oft-criticized Missouri defense rose to the challenge, rendering McFadden and Jones "almost irrelevant for much of the contest." A rushing attack that went into the game ranked fourth the nation was held to just 164 yards, 24 of which came against Missouri reserves.

With its passing attack also rendered "almost irrelevant," the

TIGERS

Tigers unleashed Tony Temple on the Hogs. All those retreating defenders "gave Temple what seemed like miles to roam." So the junior running back took off. In his final game as a Tiger, Temple set a Cotton Bowl record with 281 yards rushing; he scored four rushing touchdowns, also a bowl record.

Never in trouble, the Tigers led 28-0 in the third quarter and crushed Arkansas 38-7. The team finished No. 5 in the nation.

For every Missouri football team in every game, trouble — like a defense shutting down Chase Daniel — is gonna come. Winning or losing a game is largely determined by how a team handles the trouble that comes its way during the sixty minutes of action.

Life is no different. For each of us, trouble is gonna come. The decisive factor for us all is how we handle it. What do we do when we're in trouble?

Admittedly, some troubles are worse and are more devastating than others. From health problems to financial woes to family problems, trouble can change our lives and everything about it.

The most fearsome danger, though, lies not in what trouble can do to us physically, emotionally, or psychologically, but in its potential to affect us spiritually. Do we respond to it by turning to the profane or to the profound? Does trouble wreck our faith in God or strengthen our trust in him?

Like everything of this world, trouble is temporal; God's love and power, however, are not. In God, we have a sure and certain refuge during the troubled times of our lives.

We took what they gave us in this game.
— Chase Daniel on the Tigers' avoiding trouble in the '08 Cotton Bowl

Trouble will come and God will be there for us.

DAY 7

THE GREATEST

Read Mark 9:33-37.

"If anyone wants to be first, he must be the very last, and the servant of all" (v. 35).

It's a fact, not an opinion. Missouri's 1964 pitching staff was the greatest in the history of NCAA baseball.

Even in an age before aluminum bats when runs were dearer in all college games, what the MU pitchers did was astounding. They gave up only 19 earned runs — all season (33 games). Teams scored more unearned runs — 28 — than they did earned runs.

After a 1-3 start, MU didn't lose another game until the College World Series. They took two from St. Louis in the district playoff, which took a week to play and included a tie because of rain. They went to Omaha ranked No. 1 in the country with a 22-3-1 record.

The pitchers showed just how impressive they were in a three-game sweep of Kansas State in late April. In the first game, junior Jack Stroud struck out seventeen batters and didn't give up a hit until a scratch single in the eighth inning. Sophomore Dennis Musgraves followed up by throwing a no-hitter; only one Cat batter reached base. Keith Weber and Jim Nelson then finished off the series by combining for a five-hitter with no earned runs.

The Tigers reached the world series finals but lost to Minnesota 5-1. So did that great pitching fail in the clutch? Not at all. Only one of the Gopher runs was earned with four Tiger errors leading to four unearned runs. Stroud said years later that the weather beat Missouri. Rain delays allowed Minnesota's ace to start three games in the series, including the final game.

So was that staff *really* the greatest ever? The numbers don't lie. The earned run average for the season was 0.65, still the best in NCAA history. The second-best NCAA record is 0.81 by Long Island that same season. Nelson led MU with a 0.42 ERA and was backed up impressively by Musgraves' ERA of 0.55, Weber's 0.61, Ron Sieck at 0.82, Terry L'Ange's 1.50, and Stroud's 1.51.

They were the greatest ever.

We all want to be the greatest. The goal for the Tigers and their fans every season is the national championship. The competition at work is to be the most productive sales person on the staff or the Teacher of the Year. In other words, we define being the greatest in terms of the struggle for personal success. It's nothing new; Jesus' disciples saw greatness in the same way.

As Jesus illustrated, though, greatness in the Kingdom of God has nothing to do with the secular world's understanding of success. Rather, the greatest are those who channel their ambition toward the furtherance of Christ's kingdom through love and service, rather than their own advancement, which is a complete reversal of status and values as the world sees them.

After all, who could be greater than the person who has Jesus for a brother and God for a father? And that's every one of us.

The 1964 pitching squad is . . . the best ever in Missouri history.
                                                                    — *Rock M Nation*

**To be great for God has nothing to do
with personal advancement and everything to do
with the advancement of Christ's kingdom.**

CHEAP TRICKS

Read Acts 19:11-20.

"The evil spirit answered them, 'Jesus I know, and I know about Paul, but who are you?'" (v. 15)

When Oklahoma State tried a trick play, the Tigers were ready and snared one of the most exciting wins in their history.

On Oct. 25, 1997, MU was the underdog against the undefeated and 12th-ranked Cowboys in Stillwater. In the first half, though, it was the Tigers who looked like the unbeaten team. After OSU scored, Mizzou quarterback Corby Jones threw three touchdown passes and the ground game rushed for 221 yards. At halftime, the Tigers were in complete control with a 30-7 lead.

Man, did that all change. In the last half, the Cowboys returned the favor, putting thirty straight points on the board, the last seven coming with just under two minutes left to play. The Pokes had apparently saved themselves with a 37-30 lead.

With 18 seconds left, though, Jones hit seldom-used wide receiver Ricky Ross with a 38-yard touchdown pass. "I told [Jones] in the huddle that I was going to be there," Ross said after the game. With the extra point, the contest headed into overtime.

After both teams scored touchdowns in the first OT, Jones scampered 15 yards in the second overtime for his second touchdown of the game. The Tigers led 51-44. When State answered with a touchdown, the Cowboy coaches decided to go for the win with a two-point conversion. They called for a trick play.

TIGERS

The Pokes lined up in a really bizarre shotgun formation. The quarterback had four linemen in front of him with the six other players lined up to the left in two groups, one of two players and a second batch of four split farther out.

The Tigers weren't fooled. Junior defensive end Marquis Gibson forced the OSU quarterback to scramble. He never could get a pass off and was gang-tackled at the 2-yard line. The trick play had failed, and Missouri had a 51-50 double-overtime win.

Scam artists are everywhere and they love trick plays. An e-mail encourages you to send money to some foreign country to get rich. That guy at your front door offers to resurface your driveway at a ridiculously low price.

You've been around; you check things out before deciding. The same approach is necessary with spiritual matters, too, because false religions and bogus Christian denominations abound. The key is what any group does with Jesus. Is he the son of God, the ruler of the universe, and the only way to salvation? If not, then what the group espouses is something other than the true Word of God.

The good news about Jesus does indeed sound too good to be true, but the only catch is that there is no catch. When it comes to salvation through Jesus Christ, there's no trick lurking in the fine print. There's just the truth, right there for you to see.

When you run trick plays and they work, you're a genius. But when they don't work, folks question your sanity.

— *Bobby Bowden*

God's promises through Jesus sound too good to be true, but the only catch is that there is no catch.

PARTY ANIMALS

Read Exodus 14:26-31; 15:19-21.

"Miriam the prophetess, Aaron's sister, took a tambourine in her hand, and all the women followed her, with tambourines and dancing" (v. 15:20).

From movie stars to the Grand Canyon, a trip west was once a week-long party for the Missouri football team.

The Tigers of 1924 went 7-1 and won the Missouri Valley Conference title. Their season then received an unexpected extension when the City of Los Angeles invited them to play Southern Cal on Christmas Day. Twenty-one players, who had not practiced in two weeks, and their coaches made the journey to Hollywood.

In an age before rapid plane trips, the trip west turned into "a goodwill tour of gaping and glad-handing." The team left Columbia on Dec. 19 and was feted continually by alumni groups along the way.

The party picked up steam when the team's train arrived in the City of Angels on Dec. 23. The mayor and the USC marching band met the Tigers and paraded them to their hotel. Then the sightseeing began, highlighted by a tour of the MGM studios.

The Tigers met some of the great stars of the silent film era, including Rudolph Valentino and Lon Chaney. Swashbuckler Douglas Fairbanks personally threw a studio party for the team.

The team visited San Francisco and Catalina. On the way home, they toured the Grand Canyon and concluded their weeklong party with a New Year's Eve masquerade ball in Arizona.

The only hitch in the fairy-tale week was the ball game. The Tigers held USC scoreless the first half but then perhaps fell victim to an inadvertent miscue. A movie studio had paid a fee to film the crowded Coliseum for scenes in a silent comedy. No one told MU head coach Gwinn Henry, so while the Trojans relaxed, the Tigers "stood around, shifting nervously over the delay."

USC put a damper on the Missouri party by scoring three last-half touchdowns to win 20-7.

You know what it takes to throw a good party. You start with your closest friends, add some salsa and chips, fire up the grill and throw on some burgers and dogs, and then top it all off with the Missouri game on TV.

You probably also know that just about any old excuse will do to get people together for a celebration. All you really need is a sense that life is pretty good right now.

That's the thing about having Jesus as part of your life: He turns every day into a celebration of the good life. No matter what tragedies or setbacks life may have in store – and they will come — the heart given to Jesus will find the joy in living. That's because such a life is spent with quiet confidence in God's promise of salvation through Jesus, a confidence that inevitably bubbles up into a joy the troubles of the world cannot touch. When a life is celebrated with Jesus, the party never stops.

The weeklong trip was a gasser.
— Writer Bob Broeg on the 1924 excursion that was one long party

With Jesus, life is one big party because it becomes a celebration of victory and joy.

DAY 10

DRY RUN

Read John 4:1-15.

"Everyone who drinks this water will be thirsty again,
but whoever drinks the water I give him will never thirst.
Indeed, the water I give him will become in him a spring
of water welling up to eternal life" (vv. 13-14).

Fifteen minutes of fireworks. That's all it took to end a drought of biblical proportions, one that stretched across twenty-five years.

On Oct. 11, 2003, the Tigers hosted Nebraska, seeking their first win over the Huskers since 1978. The odds of MU's avoiding its twenty-fifth straight loss in the series didn't look good. Nebraska was ranked tenth in the nation and was undefeated at 5-0. Its defense led the nation in stinginess.

Sure enough, barely six minutes into the game, that defense set up a touchdown for a quick 7-0 lead. But as All-Big 12 center A.J. Ricker said after the game, "Everyone fought . . . everyone." The Tigers fought back to lead 14-10 at halftime.

In the third quarter, though, Nebraska asserted itself, grinding out two touchdowns to take a 24-14 lead into the final period. It sure looked as though the drought would continue.

"But instead of wilting, Mizzou untapped a reservoir of resolve." On the first play of the fourth quarter, the fifteen minutes of fireworks began when quarterback Brad Smith broke loose around his left end for a 39-yard scoring run. After a Nebraska fumble, the Tigers pulled off a successful fake field goal. Holder

TIGERS

Sonny Riccio, the backup quarterback, lofted a strike to tight end Victor Sesay in the end zone. With 11:21 to play, Mizzou led 28-24, and "the big gathering was in a frenzy."

It got even more frenzied as the Tigers drove for another touchdown before defensive end Zach Ville nabbed an interception and lugged it to the Husker 7. Smith scored again, and MU led 41-24, the final score.

The drought had ended, and "the celebration that had been on hold for 25 years finally began."

You can walk across that river you boated on in the spring. The city's put all neighborhoods on water restriction. That beautiful lawn you fertilized and seeded will turn a sickly, pale green and may lapse all the way to brown. Somebody wrote "Wash Me" on the rear window of your truck. It didn't strike you as funny.

The sun bakes everything, including the concrete. The earth itself seems exhausted, just barely hanging on. It's a drought.

It's the way a soul that shuts God out looks.

God instilled the physical sensation of thirst in us to warn us of our body's need for water. He also gave us a spiritual thirst that can be quenched only by his presence in our lives. Without God, we are like tumbleweeds, dried out and windblown, offering the illusion of life where there is only death.

Living water — the water of life — is readily available in Jesus. We may drink our fill, and thus we slake our thirst and end our soul's drought — forever.

It hasn't sunk in, really. Pretty amazing.
— Gary Pinkel on ending the drought vs. Nebraska

Our soul thirsts for God's refreshing presence.

DAY 11

MIDDLE OF NOWHERE

Read Genesis 28:10-22.

"When Jacob awoke from his sleep, he thought, 'Surely the Lord is in this place, and I was not aware of it'" (v. 16).

Not a single traffic light and only one restaurant. The kids hung out at the car wash. And right there in the middle of nowhere was the greatest sharpshooter in MU women's basketball history.

Morgan Eye grew up in Montrose. "Population: 384," she once said when asked to describe her hometown, which sits unobtrusively some 80 miles southeast of Kansas City. She had twelve in her graduating class. For fun, Eye and her friends would gather at "The Lot," which was the parking lot of a car wash. They'd throw a football or ride around. "Cruising the town," Eye called it.

Mostly, though, Eye shot a basketball. Her father laid a concrete slab in the backyard with plans to put a building on it. "It never happened," her mother said. Instead, that half-court-sized slab with no painted lines became Eye's personal basketball court. There she spent most of her time working on her game.

Eye never had a shooting coach and didn't play AAU ball. Her odd shot is proof of that. Instead of stepping forward to let fly with a long-range shot, she slides her left foot back just before she shoots. "We joke about my footwork," she said. "It's kind of my trademark. I can't explain it."

The recruiters evidently couldn't find Montrose, so Eye sent videos to Kansas, Kansas State, and Missouri. MU coach Robin

TIGERS

Pingeton saw a kid who "maybe didn't quite have the athleticism we were looking for," but "she could absolutely knock the bottom out of it." At the time, Pingeton said, "We couldn't throw the ball in the ocean." She offered Eye a scholarship.

What she got was a star who set a school and SEC record as a sophomore in 2012-13 with 112 three-pointers. By the end of her junior season, she had nailed 283 treys, already a school record.

Morgan Eye, the sharpshooter from the middle of nowhere, put Montrose on the map.

Ever been fishing in Tunas? Met the girls in Hilda or just down the road in Ava? Made progress in Advance? They are among the many small communities, some of them nothing more than crossroads, that dot the Missouri countryside. They seem to be in the middle of nowhere, the type of place where Morgan Eye could be found in her backyard shooting a basketball. They're just hamlets we zip through on our way to somewhere important.

But don't be misled; those villages are special and wonderful places. That's because God is in Plato and Lemons just as he is in Columbia, downtown St. Louis, and Springfield. Even when you are far off the roads well traveled, you are with God.

As Jacob discovered to his dismay on one rather astounding morning, the middle of nowhere is, in fact, holy ground – because God is there.

She's a sweet-talking country girl who was raised on a bean farm in a town that has no traffic lights and one restaurant.
— Sportswriter Ross Dellenger on Morgan Eye

**No matter how far off the beaten path you travel,
you are still on holy ground because God is there.**

A RIPE OLD AGE

Read Psalm 92.

"[The righteous] will still bear fruit in old age, they will stay fresh and green, proclaiming, 'The Lord is upright'" (vv. 14-15).

The old man was back.

On March 6, 2012, offensive tackle Elvis Fisher returned to the Missouri practice field, and he was overjoyed to be there despite a steady diet of ribbing from his teammates. In August 2011, Fisher had torn a tendon in his left knee during practice, ending his senior season before it ever started. His loss was a big blow to the Tiger offense. He had started all forty games at left tackle from 2008-10 and had been a First-Team Freshman All-America.

One of the most likeable and engaging guys on the roster took the injury hard. "I wasn't a nice guy to be around," he said. But the 6-5, 300-lb. veteran worked hard to rehab and caught a break when the NCAA granted him an extra hardship year.

So on the first day of spring practice in 2012, he was back, a sixth-year senior with the owner of a hairline that had steadily faded since he first put a big foot on the MU campus. For the second year in a row, he was the oldest man on the Tiger football team, and his bald head helped him look the part.

His teammates didn't let him forget it. They "ask me, 'What was it like to play in the Big Eight?'" Fisher said. "Or, 'How did you like playing for Dan Devine?'"

TIGERS

"You mean Grandpa?" remarked fellow tackle Justin Britt. "He knows he's old. He looks in the mirror and sees it every day. He has kids and has grandkids he doesn't even tell us about."

All kidding aside, Fisher's return was a big boost to the Tiger offensive line. The two-time team captain stepped back into the left tackle spot for a fourth, if delayed, season as a starter in 2012. "With Elvis back . . . [it's] a huge help for us," said head coach Gary Pinkel.

Even if he was the team's resident senior citizen.

To consider someone old by age 23 as Elvis Fisher was during most of the 2012 season is rather extreme even for our youth-obsessed culture. Still, we don't like to admit — even to ourselves — that we're not as young as we used to be.

So we keep plastic surgeons in business, dye our hair, buy cases of those miracle wrinkle-reducing creams, and redouble our efforts in the gym. Sometimes, though, we just have to face up to the truth the mirror tells us: We're getting older every day.

It's really all right, though, because aging and old age are part of the natural cycle of our lives, which was God's idea in the first place. God's conception of the golden years, though, doesn't include unlimited close encounters with a rocking chair and nothing more. God expects us to serve him as we are able all the days of our life. Those who serve God flourish no matter their age because the energizing power of God is in them.

I've gotten old-man jokes for a while because I've been bald forever.
— Elvis Fisher in the spring of 2012

Servants of God don't ever retire; they keep working until they get the ultimate promotion.

IN THE BAD TIMES

Read Philippians 1:3-14.

"What has happened to me has really served to advance the gospel. . . . Because of my chains, most of the brothers in the Lord have been encouraged to speak the word of God more courageously and fearlessly" (vv. 12, 14).

Talk about your bad times: no father and a mother on drugs, no one to provide food or clothes, three years in the sixth grade, time spent in a mental hospital and in a youth home for criminal offenders. And then William Moore turned to Jesus and sports.

Moore "seemed destined to be engulfed in the cycle of hopelessness" that enveloped the area in which he grew up. So spoke his pastor, Jamie Jones. "He never had anything."

Moore's father was not in his life; his mother was a drug addict. He often never knew whether he'd eat or not and sometimes had to borrow clothes and shoes from friends. He flunked the sixth grade twice. His mother put him in a mental hospital for observation and in a home for youthful offenders for a year.

After being released from the youth home, the more mature Moore was still adrift and disillusioned. In the midst of the chaos around him, however, he realized that to avoid doing the wrong things, he had to immerse himself in constructive ones.

First of all, that meant the church. "He began to do so many positive things that people wanted to cling to him," Jones said. That also meant athletics. Even after Moore received a scholarship to Missouri, Jones said, "They said he'd never complete school. They said he'd be in the penitentiary."

They were wrong. Moore became a star. As a junior safety in 2007, he set a school record with eight interceptions. He was All-Big 12 and All-America. He went on to become a starter with the Atlanta Falcons; in 2013, he sighed a $32-million contract.

At Missouri, Moore found himself pausing not to reflect on the bad times, but why his life was so full of blessings.

Loved ones die. You're downsized. Your biopsy looks cancerous. Your spouse could be having an affair. Hard, tragic times are as much a part of life as breath. Just ask William Moore.

This applies to Christians too. Christianity is not the equivalent of a Get-out-of-Jail-Free card, granting us a lifelong exemption from either the least or the worst pain the world has to offer. While Jesus promises us he will be there to lead us through the valleys, he never promises that we will not enter them.

The question thus becomes how you handle the bad times. You can buckle to your knees in despair and cry, "Why me?" Or you can hit your knees in prayer and ask, "What do I do with this?"

Setbacks and tragedies are opportunities to reveal and to develop true character and abiding faith. Your faithfulness — not your skipping merrily along through life without pain — is what reveals the depth of your love for God.

He was around so much destruction that he couldn't do nothing but fall into the shadows.
— Pastor Jamie Jones on William Moore's bad times growing up

Faithfulness to God requires faith even in
— especially in — the bad times.

DAY 14

HIDEAWAY

Read Psalm 139:1-12.

"Where can I go from your Spirit? Where can I flee from your presence?" (v. 7)

A Missouri coach who would eventually be elected to the College Football Hall of Fame grew so tired of athletic fame that he changed his name and virtually went into hiding.

Pat O'Dea became Mizzou's head football coach in 1902. An Irishman from Australia, he came to the U.S. in search of an older brother who coached at Wisconsin. O'Dea was a rugby player back home, and his feats as a kicker at Wisconsin became the stuff of fable. He once punted 110 yards into the Minnesota end zone and also sailed a ball 100 yards in the air against Yale. Against Northwestern in 1898, he drop-kicked a field goal 62 yards "on a muddy field and with a heavy ball." A sprinter, he returned a kickoff 90 yards for a touchdown against Boston College. He also kicked four field goals in that game.

After a season coaching at Notre Dame, O'Dea came to Missouri and coached the '02 team to a 5-3 record. During the 27-0 win over Washington University in St. Louis, one of the Bears finally had enough of what he perceived as unfavorable officiating decisions and kicked the only game ball into the stands. "Game called on account of lost ball."

After one season in Columbia, O'Dea left and went to California. There he became something of a mystery man, dropping

TIGERS

completely out of the public's consciousness. He began a law practice in 1906 before rumors had it he was killed during World War I while serving with an Australian unit.

In 1934, though, a sportswriter created a stir when he wrote that "Charles Mitchell," an accountant for a lumber company, was actually Pat O'Dea in hiding. Tired of being a famous ex-athlete, he had changed his name and disappeared. He died in 1962, one day after he was elected to the College Football Hall of Fame.

Like Pat O'Dea, we often believe we can hide from others. You may have had a hideout when you were a child. You may have a place in your home that's all yours, a spot where you can hide for a brief time and enjoy the solitude of being apart from the world. But even in that hideout and even in that personal place, you are not and never have been alone. God is there.

We do and believe many foolish things over the course of our lives, but little is as ridiculous as believing we can hide from God or that God won't notice what we're doing, saying, or thinking.

Here's the bad news: God is omnipresent; he is everywhere, all the time. We can't hide from him.

On the other hand, here's the good news: God is omnipresent; he is everywhere, all the time. We can't hide from him. God, thus, is always with us, and so is his comforting presence, his boundless love, and his saving grace.

God sees, God knows, God loves.

Apparently, O'Dea had just become tired of being a football celebrity.
— Writer Brian Peterson on why Pat O'Dea went into hiding

**We can't hide from God's presence, which means
we also can't escape his love and his grace.**

KNOW-IT-ALLS

Read Matthew 13:10-17.

"The knowledge of the secrets of the kingdom of heaven has been given to you" (v. 11).

There they were, the members of the 2009 Missouri soccer team, celebrating a Big 12 championship largely because their head coach had decided he had a lot to learn.

Bryan Blitz headed up the MU soccer program when it began in 1996. It enjoyed some early success, including a berth in the 1999 NCAA Tournament. After that, though, "Missouri seemingly found its station as a member of the Big 12's middle class." Until, that is, the 2004-06 seasons when the program "dropped below the poverty line" with a 7-21-2 record in conference play.

After the '06 season, Blitz figured he needed to go back to school. He turned to North Carolina coach Anson Dorrance, who had won nineteen national championships. Blitz applied what he had learned; among the major changes was the adoption of UNC's attacking style by using a third forward instead of a defender.

Success was immediate. The 2007 squad made the NCAA Tournament. The '08 team won the Big 12 Tournament and returned to the Big Dance. Then on a rainy Sunday afternoon, Oct. 25, the 2009 team made history. The Tigers whipped Nebraska 5-0 to win the league championship. The only other MU team to accomplish that feat was the 1997 softball squad. In fact, the trophy Blitz held to signify the championship was actually that of the softball team.

TIGERS

Over the old inscription, the head coach taped a scrap of paper heralding his team's first-ever soccer title.

The historic win marked the realization of what the team's six seniors had believed they could accomplish when they had committed to Missouri. Bree Thornton, Crystal Wagner, Meghan Pfeiffer, Michelle Collins, Tasha Dittamore, and Kristin Andrighetto had all signed on back when the program was struggling, back before their head coach went back to school.

As Bryan Blitz's career demonstrates, we can never know too much. We once thought our formal education ended when we entered the workplace, but now we have constant training sessions, conferences, and seminars to keep us current whether our expertise is in auto mechanics or medicine. Many areas require graduate degrees now as we scramble to stay abreast of new discoveries and information. And still we never know it all.

In no other aspect of our life, however, is the paucity of our knowledge more stark than it is when we consider God. We will never know even a fraction of all there is to apprehend about the creator of the universe — with one exception. God has revealed all we need to know about the kingdom of heaven to ensure our salvation. He has opened to us great and eternal secrets.

All we need to know about getting into Heaven is in the Bible. With God, ignorance is no excuse and knowledge is salvation.

Dude, remember where we were freshman year?
— Michelle Collins to fellow senior Bree Thornton after beating NU

When it comes to our salvation, we can indeed know it all because God has revealed to us everything we need to know.

TEST CASE

Read Genesis 39.

"But while Joseph was there in the prison, the Lord was with him" (vv. 20b, 21a).

Head coach Gary Pinkel called it Maty Mauk's final exam of the fall semester — and he aced it.

The redshirt freshman quarterback's status as the backup to senior star James Franklin changed suddenly on Oct. 12, 2013, when Franklin left the Georgia game with a shoulder sprain. With no warning or preparation, Mauk "was thrust into the cauldron of a game slipping away at Georgia's Sanford Stadium."

He passed what was called the "seat-of-his-pants crash landing" that storied afternoon in Athens, but that was only the beginning of Mauk's testing time. It would be six weeks and four more games before Franklin would return.

Mauk would be graded not necessarily on how well he played but whether he performed well enough to keep alive Missouri's dreams of a big season. He quarterbacked the Tigers to wins over Florida (his first career start) and Tennessee that set up his final exam against Kentucky on Nov. 9.

The Wildcats offered the sternest test of all. The MU coaches had anticipated that Kentucky's defense would spend the afternoon backpedaling into safe coverage. When Mauk looked over the defense for his first snap, though, he saw a line of scrimmage that was loaded with defenders; the cornerbacks were up tight against the wide receivers. As offensive coordinator Josh Henson put it, the Cats were saying that Mauk would have to beat them.

He did. He completed 17 of 28 passes for 203 yards and tied Chase Daniel's school record by throwing five touchdown passes. Missouri won 48-17.

Mauk finished his month-long test throwing for 951 yards and 10 TDs. Three times he was the SEC Freshman of the Week. Most of all, he kept the dream alive. Test grade? A+

Life often seems to be just one battery of tests after another: high-school and college final exams, college entrance exams, the driver's license test, professional certification exams.

But it is the tests in our lives that don't involve paper and pen that often demand the most of us. That is, like Maty Mauk in 2013, we regularly run headlong into challenges, obstacles, and barriers that test our abilities and our persistence, and sometimes — as it was with Joseph in prison in Egypt — our faith.

Life itself is one long test, which means some parts are bound to be hard. In fact, the difficult circumstances of our lives most directly test and build our character and our faith.

Viewing life as an ongoing exam may help you preserve your sanity, your perspective, and your faith when you find yourself tested. After all, God is the proctor, but he isn't neutral. He even gave you the answer you need to pass life's test with flying colors; that answer is "Jesus."

With that answer, you don't get a grade; you get Heaven.

Big picture, [Maty Mauk's] 30-day trial was a major success.
— Sportswriter Joe Walljasper

Life is a test that God wants you to ace.

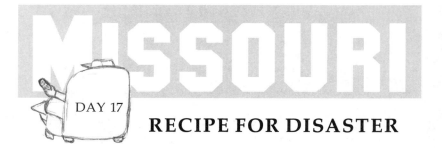

RECIPE FOR DISASTER

Read Luke 21:5-11, 25-28.

"There will be great earthquakes, famines and pestilences in various places, and fearful events and great signs from heaven" (v. 11).

If Dan Devine lacked a sense of humor, he never would have come to Missouri." That's because his first visit to Columbia was an unmitigated disaster.

After one season as the Tigers' head coach, Frank Broyles took off for Arkansas before Christmas 1957. As he began his search, AD Don Faurot recalled a conversation he had had with Michigan State head coach Duffy Daugherty about "a bright young coach" at Arizona State. That coach was Dan Devine.

Faurot needed three phone conversations to convince Devine to come from Tempe, Ariz., for a visit. The trip turned out to be noteworthy, but for all the wrong reasons.

During the flight, a stewardess spilled hot chocolate on Devine. The plane developed engine trouble and arrived in Kansas City six hours late. On the ride to Columbia, Faurot ran out of fuel and had to hitch a ride to a gas station with a trucker. So Devine — who was dressed for the warmth of Arizona and not the cold of Missouri — shivered alone in the car in the middle of the night and wondered what in the world he was doing there.

The trip didn't get much better when Faurot returned with some gas. They rested a bit at the AD's home and then hit the road early for Rolla where the board of curators was meeting. It was a "fog-shrouded, winding, narrow highway" that left Devine "wondering only whether I'll live to see my family again."

He did, and Faurot led the charge that ultimately sold Devine on Columbia and the university, despite the disastrous trip.

We live in a world that seems to be either struck by one disaster after another or is the home of several ongoing and seemingly permanent disasters. Admittedly, they're on a much more serious scale than a lousy trip to Columbia.

Earthquakes virtually obliterate an entire nation; volcanoes erupt and change the climate; children around the world starve to death every day. Floods devastate cities and shatter lives; oil pollutes our oceans and seashores. Can we even count the number of wars that are going on at any one time?

This apparently unending litany of disaster is enough to make us all give up hope. Maybe — but not for the followers of Jesus Christ. The truth is that Jesus' disciples should find reassurance of their ultimate hope in the world's constant disasters because this is exactly what Jesus said would happen.

These disasters indicate that the time of our redemption is drawing near. How near is up to God to decide. Nevertheless, this is a season of hope and great promise for those of the faith.

There I sat in the dark at 2 a.m. wearing a coat too thin, shivering, and wondering what in heck I was doing in Missouri in the first place.
— Dan Devine on his 'recruitment' trip to Columbia

**Jesus told us what to do when disaster threatens
to overwhelm us and our world: 'Stand up
and lift up your heads.'**

CALLING IT QUITS

Read Numbers 13:25-14:4.

"The men who had gone up with him said, 'We can't attack those people; they are stronger than we are'" (v. 13:31).

Two things we can know for sure about Chase Patton: He was not a star at MU and he is not a quitter. Oh, and he was good enough to land on the cover of *ESPN The Magazine*.

Patton was a high-school All-American quarterback who committed to MU and arrived on campus in 2004 knowing he would play behind Brad Smith for two years. What he hadn't counted on was Chase Daniel and Blaine Gabbert. Patton wound up "playing second fiddle to them all."

"Most often, quarterbacks at [Patton's] level would go on to transfer," said head coach Gary Pinkel. Patton thought about it, but relied on his family and friends and his faith and honored his commitment to Missouri. He memorized all 27 verses of the first chapter of James with its admonition that our faith will be tested and we must persevere.

Patton never once mentioned a transfer to his coaches. "If my role was to be a backup quarterback, I was going to be the best backup quarterback I could be," he said.

In 2008, Patton's senior year, *ESPN* contacted him for a story in the magazine about overlooked backup quarterbacks. Patton figured he would rate a small, insignificant snippet. Instead, he

TIGERS

wound up on the cover of the magazine, which suggested he would make a better pro quarterback than Daniel would.

Patton threw only one touchdown pass at Missouri. On Nov. 8, 2008, Senior Day, Patton made it into the 41-24 win over Kansas State in the fourth quarter. He completed a pass to wide receiver Jared Perry, and Perry broke two tackles and scored.

If Patton needed any affirmation about how his teammates felt about him, he received it at the end-of-season banquet in 2008. His fellow Tigers voted the quarterback who didn't quit on them the team's Most Inspirational Player.

Remember when you quit a high-school sports team or that night you bailed out of a relationship? Sometimes quitting is the most sensible way to minimize your losses, so you may well at times in your life give up on something or someone.

In your relationship with God, however, you should remember the people of Israel, who quit when the Promised Land was theirs for the taking. They forgot one fact of life you never should: God never gives up on you.

That means you should never, ever give up on God. No matter how tired or discouraged you get, no matter that it seems your prayers aren't getting through to God, no matter what — quitting on God is not an option.

He is preparing a blessing for you, and in his time, he will bring it to fruition — if you don't quit on him.

He's not a quitter. He's a great person, a great kid.
— MU quarterbacks coach David Yost on Chase Patton

Whatever else you give up on in your life, don't give up on God; he will never ever give up on you.

THE PREDICTION

Read Isaiah 53.

"But he was pierced for our transgressions, he was crushed for our iniquities; the punishment that brought us peace was upon him, and by his wounds we are healed" (v. 5).

Prior to the 1939 Nebraska game, Missouri quarterback Paul Christman made a bold, cocky prediction about his performance.

From 1938-40, "Pitchin' Paul" led the Tigers to a 20-8 record with the Big Six Title in '39. He was three-time All-Conference and twice All-America. He finished third in the Heisman Trophy voting in '39. In 1940, he led the nation with 1,131 yards passing and thirteen touchdown passes. He still ranks tenth in MU history with 3,882 yards of total offense. His jersey number 44 has been retired.

The '39 Tigers won four of their first five games but were still the underdogs in the showdown with unbeaten Nebraska on Nov. 4 for what amounted to the league title. The morning of the game Christman and the other Catholics on the team attended Mass. After the service, Christman stopped by the *Columbia Tribune* offices next door, tapped writer Bob Broeg on the shoulder, grinned, and whispered rather loudly, "I'll give you a scoop, kid. I'll pass those bums out of the stadium by the half."

Broeg laughed in response.

Christman made good on his prediction, throwing three touchdown passes in the first half to stake the Tigers to a 20-6 lead. At the break, Broeg spread the word around the press box about Christman's "jocular pregame boast." It "was too good to keep," Broeg explained.

After delivering on his prediction, Christman led the Tigers to a 27-13 win, the only loss the Huskers would suffer. Missouri wound up in the 1940 Orange Bowl. Years later, Christman would shake his head and ask, "How could I have said those things?"

In our jaded age, we have pretty much relegated prophecy to dark rooms in which mysterious women peer into crystal balls or clasp our sweaty palms while uttering some vague generalities. At best, we understand a prophet as someone who predicts future events as Paul Christman did against Nebraska.

Within the pages of the Bible, though, we encounter something radically different. A prophet is a messenger from God, one who relays divine revelation to others.

Prophets seem somewhat foreign to us because in one very real sense the age of prophecy is over. In the name of Jesus, we have access to God through our prayers and through scripture. In searching for God's will for our lives, we seek divine revelation. We may speak only for ourselves and not for the greater body of Christ, but we do not need a prophet to discern what God would have us do. We need faith in the one whose birth, life, and death fulfilled more than 300 Bible prophecies.

The Merry Magician called his shot.
— *Bob Broeg on Paul Christman's Nebraska prediction*

**Persons of faith continuously seek a word
from God for their lives.**

THE PREDICTION   39

THE CHALLENGE

Read Matthew 4:12-25.

"Come, follow me," Jesus said (v. 19).

Missouri once challenged Kansas to a one-game showdown for the conference and probably the national championship — and the Jayhawks backed down.

The Tigers opened the 1921-22 basketball season as the two-time defending champions of the Missouri Valley Conference. Gone, however, were scoring machine George Williams, a two-time All-America and 1921's national player of the year, and two other starters, Pidge Browning and Leslie Wacker.

All-American Herb Bunker was back, though. The four-sport letterman "proceeded to become a defensive presence of nearly mythic proportions." Head coach Craig Ruby also found a star in forward Arthur "Bun" Browning, an All-America in 1922 and '23.

An early showdown came in the sixth game of the season as 5-0 MU met undefeated Kansas and won easily 35-25. The Tigers were 13-0 when the teams met again, and Kansas got its revenge with a 26-16 win. Both teams finished 15-1 in the conference.

Dissatisfied, Missouri's athletic committee challenged Kansas to a one-game playoff at a neutral site. Kansas declined, using academic integrity as its excuse. "We have kept in mind the fundamental that the university does not exist for athletics," the chancellor sniffed. The season "has been long and arduous enough," he said, adding that Missouri could wait until next year. Not

TIGERS

surprisingly, the response was met with derision in Columbia.

As it turned out, the game would have been for the national championship. In 1936, the Helms Foundation, for its own unexplained reasons, named Kansas 1922's mythical champion. Later, historian Patrick Premo researched college basketball's early seasons and declared the Tigers to be 1922's best.

Since the challenge went unanswered, no one knows for sure.

Like the MU athletic teams every time they take the field or the court, we are challenged daily. Life is a testing ground; God intentionally set it up that way. If we are to grow in character, confidence, and perseverance, and if we are to make a difference in the world, we must meet challenges head-on. Few things in life are as boring and as destructive to our sense of self-worth as a job that doesn't offer any challenges.

Our faith life is the same way. The moment we answered Jesus' call to "Come, follow me," we took on the most difficult challenge we will ever face. We are called to be holy by walking in Jesus' footsteps in a world that seeks to render our Lord irrelevant and his influence negligible. The challenge Jesus places before us is to put our faith and our trust in him and not in ourselves or the transitory values of the secular world.

Daily walking in Jesus' footsteps is a challenge, but the path takes us all the way right up to the gates of Heaven — and then right on through.

Some deemed KU's explanation an 'alibi.'
— Writer Michael Atchison in True Sons

To accept Jesus as Lord is to joyfully take on the challenge of living a holy life in an unholy world.

VIRTUAL REALITY

Read Habakkuk 1:2-11.

"Why do you make me look at injustice? Why do you tolerate wrong? Destruction and violence are before me; there is strife, and conflict abounds" (v. 3).

A reasonable person might well assume that the University of Missouri used a jungle cat as the basis for its mascot. After all, its school colors are black and gold, same as a Bengal tiger. Oh, but things are not what they seem.

MU seized its collective nickname not from a species but from an event. As the Civil War raged, bushwhackers pillaged central Missouri. "The people of central Missouri lived in fear as [William T. 'Bloody Bill'] Anderson moved from county to county." After a massacre and looting in Centralia, Anderson and his men were reported on their way to Columbia.

On Aug. 1, 1864, a mass meeting at the Boone County Courthouse was held to organize a home-guard militia of every able-bodied man in the county. They called themselves the Boone County Tigers to "indicate the fierce and desperate nature of [the] members." What resulted provided "one of the few humorous anecdotes from an otherwise grim and bloody year."

The Tigers built a blockhouse in the middle of the street at the corner of Eighth and Broadway. They stocked it with food, water, supplies, and ammunition and offered refuge to women and children.

TIGERS

The raid never came. The Tigers never left Columbia and they never fought. One historian declared they could more accurately have been dubbed the "Snow-White Lambs." He described them as harmless and gentle with "an aversion to the smell of 'villainous saltpeter.'" The Tigers wound up having "barrels of fun" since "it was such jolly sport to shirk duty, such as standing picket."

Soon after Missouri's first football team was formed in 1890, the athletic committee chose the nickname "Tigers" in recognition of the fighting spirit of Columbia's Civil War militia.

Sometimes in life, reality — including mascots — isn't what it seems. In our violent and convulsive times, we must confront the possibility of a new reality: that we are helpless in the face of anarchy; that injustice, destruction, and violence are pandemic in and symptomatic of our modern age. Anarchy seems to be winning, and the system of standards, values, and institutions we have cherished appears to be crumbling while we watch.

But we should not be deceived or disheartened. God is in fact the arch-enemy of chaos, the creator of order and goodness and the architect of all of history. God is in control. We often misinterpret history as the record of mankind's accomplishments — which it isn't — rather than the unfolding of God's plan — which it is. That plan has a clearly defined end: God will make everything right. In that day reality will be exactly what it seems to be.

They could hardly be called 'Tigers,' having in view the fitness of terms.
— Historian William Switzler on Columbia's home guard

The forces of good and decency often seem
helpless before evil's power, but don't be fooled:
God is in control and will set things right.

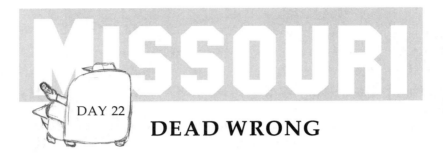

DEAD WRONG

Read Matthew 26:14-16; 27:1-10.

"When Judas, who had betrayed him, saw that Jesus was condemned, he was seized with remorse" (v. 27:3).

Roger Wehrli figured his days of playing football were over after his last high-school game. Boy, was he wrong.

Wehrli was a star in high school, playing football, basketball, and baseball, and running track. The problem was he did it all in King City, which boasted a population of about 1,000 people. Because his school had so few boys, "The game we played at King City wasn't very sophisticated," Wehrli said. Thus, he set his sights on a baseball scholarship at Northwest Missouri State.

When Wehrli led his small school to a state title in track, he caught the attention of Missouri defensive backfield coach Clay Cooper. Cooper watched some crude 8mm film and then convinced head coach Dan Devine that Wehrli had potential as a defensive back. Missouri gave its last football scholarship in 1965 to Wehrli with the stipulation that he play baseball also — in case the football thing didn't work out.

Baseball disappeared from the radar when Wehrli earned a starting position as a sophomore in 1966. "He was an instant hit." In his second game, he had two interceptions in a 21-14 defeat of Illinois.

In 1967, Wehrli began showing off his versatility, excelling as a kick returner. He returned a punt 64 yards for a touchdown against SMU (a 21-0 win); he also went 96 yards with the opening kickoff in the 23-7 whipping of Iowa State.

Wehrli's "senior season was one for the ages." He led the nation in punt returns on his way to setting eight school special teams and defensive records, including his three interceptions against OSU. He earned All-Big Eight and All-American honors.

Dead wrong about his playing days ending with high school, Wehrli went on to a pro career. He was inducted into the MU Hall of Fame in 1990 and the Pro Football Hall of Fame in 2007.

There's wrong, there's dead wrong, and there's Judas wrong. We've all been wrong in our lives, but we can at least honestly ease our conscience by telling ourselves we'll never be as wrong as Judas was. A close examination of Judas' actions, however, reveals that we can indeed replicate in our own lives the mistake Judas made that drove him to suicidal despair.

Judas ultimately regretted his betrayal of our Lord, but his sorrow and remorse, however boundless, could not save him. His attempt to undo his initial wrong was futile because he tried to fix everything himself rather than turning to God in repentance and begging for mercy.

While we can't literally betray Jesus to his enemies as Judas did, we can match Judas' failure in our own lives by not turning to God in Jesus' name and asking for forgiveness for our sins. In that case, we ultimately will be as dead wrong as Judas was.

I felt I was through with football and I regretted that.
— Roger Wehrli after playing his last high-school football game

A sin is the first wrong; failing to ask God
for forgiveness of it is the second.

A LONG SHOT

Read Matthew 9:9-13.

"[Jesus] saw a man named Matthew sitting at the tax collector's booth. 'Follow me,' he told him, and Matthew got up and followed him" (v. 9).

Jeff Wolfert broke his hip in the only high-school football game he ever kicked in. Thus, he was certainly a long shot to become a college kicker, let alone the greatest in school history.

Wolfert excelled in soccer and diving in high school in Kansas. In 2003, his senior season, he decided to give up soccer and try kicking a football. In his first game, trying to drive the ball into the end zone on a kickoff, he broke his hip and was sidelined for the rest of the season.

After graduation, he enrolled at Missouri on a diving scholarship and was an all-conference diver as a freshman. "I still had a dream of playing football," Wolfert said. "I knew that I was good at kicking, . . . [but[my experience . . . on a team was so limited, I had no idea if there was actually something worthwhile there."

When Missouri head coach Gary Pinkel issued an all-points bulletin for a kicker in 2005, Wolfert decided to try out. Tiger kicking coach David Yost watched him kick and offered him a walk-on spot. To kick for the football team, however, Wolfert had to turn his back on his diving scholarship and career. "I really had to give up what I loved," Wolfert said, but he did it.

He was a football redshirt in 2005, and then in 2006 he set

about making history. In three seasons as the Tiger kicker, he never missed an extra point (185 for 185). He set the school's single season and career scoring records (133 and 362 points). An Academic All-Big 12 honoree, Wolfert was First Team All-Big 12 in 2007 and '08. He received a full scholarship in April 2007.

How did this true long shot — since he never kicked in high school — become the greatest kicker in Missouri history? "He works very hard at it," quarterback Chase Daniel explained.

Like Jeff Wolfert, Matthew the tax collector was a long shot. In his case, he was an unlikely person to be a confidant of the Son of God. While we may not get all warm and fuzzy about the IRS, our government's revenue agents are nothing like Matthew and his ilk. He bought a franchise, paying the Roman Empire for the privilege of extorting, bullying, and stealing everything he could from his own people. Tax collectors of the time were "despicable, vile, unprincipled scoundrels."

And yet, Jesus said only two words to this lowlife: "Follow me." Jesus knew that this long shot would make an excellent disciple.

It's the same with us. While we may not be quite as vile as Matthew was, none of us can stand before God with our hands clean and our hearts pure. We are all impossibly long shots to enter God's Heaven. That is, until we do what Matthew did: get up and follow Jesus.

I went 1 for 2 in extra points and on my first kickoff I broke my hip as I was swinging through the ball. Season over.
— Long-shot college kicker Jeff Wolfert on his high-school football career

**Jesus changes us from being long shots
to enter God's Kingdom to being sure things.**

HOW WE LEAVE

Read 2 Kings 2:1-12.

"A chariot of fire and horses of fire appeared and separated the two of them, and Elijah went up to heaven in a whirlwind" (v. 11).

For a long time it seemed downright impossible, but Henry Josey left Missouri on top.

When Kendial Lawrence, the projected starter at running back, broke his leg in September 2011, Josey, a sophomore, moved up. He became a star. By the time of the meeting with Texas on Nov. 12, he had rushed for more than 100 yards in four straight games, scored nine touchdowns, and was fifth in the nation in total yards.

Against the Longhorns, however, at the end of a run along the sideline, Josey suffered what MU trainer Rex Sharp called "the worst knee injury in athletics I've ever seen." In effect, Josey's left knee was shredded, most of its working parts simply torn up. He had three surgeries from November 2011 to May 2012. The last surgery came because doctors had to wait six months for the rest of his knee to heal before they could repair the ACL.

Despite the many naysayers who said his injury was too severe for him ever to play again, Josey never wavered in his belief that he would be back. He was. He was redshirted in 2012, but was in the starting lineup for the 2013 opener on Aug. 31 against Murray State, a 58-14 romp. He broke off a 68-yard TD run.

Josey finished the season with 1,166 yards rushing, which left him as the No.-5 rusher in Mizzou history with 2,771 yards. He ripped off a 57-yard go-ahead touchdown run in the 28-21 win over Texas A&M that clinched the SEC Eastern Division title. Then in the Cotton Bowl, Josey, the game's offensive MVP, put MU ahead for good in the 41-31 win over Oklahoma State with a 16-yard touchdown run late in the fourth quarter.

It was his final college play. Leaving on top as few expected he would, Josey declared for the NFL draft after the season ended.

Like Henry Josey, who admitted his knee injury played a big part in his decision to turn pro, and Elijah, we can't always choose the exact circumstances under which we leave.

You probably haven't always chosen the moves you've made in your life. Perhaps your company transferred you. A landlord didn't renew your lease. An elderly parent needed your care.

Sometimes the only choice we have about leaving is the manner in which we go, whether or not we depart with style and grace. Our exit from life is the same way. Unless we usurp God's authority over life and death, we can't choose how we die, just how we handle it. Perhaps the most frustrating aspect of dying is that we have at most very little control over the process. As with our birth, our death is in God's hands. We finally must surrender to his will even if we have spent a lifetime refusing to do so.

We do, however, control our destination. How we leave isn't up to us; where we spend eternity is — and that depends on our relationship with Jesus.

You always want to go out when you're on top.
> *— Henry Josey, deciding to turn pro after the Cotton Bowl*

How you go isn't up to you; where you go is.

DAY 25

A SECOND CHANCE

Read John 7:53-8:11.

*"'Then neither do I condemn you,' Jesus declared. 'Go
now and leave your life of sin'" (v. 8:11).*

After giving up gymnastics because it wasn't fun anymore,
Sarah Shire decided to give the sport a second chance. All she did
was lead Missouri to the greatest season in the program's history.

Shire began tumbling when she was 3 years old, and from the
first she was good. As she grew up, her parents supported her by
moving to Sweet Springs to be close to a gymnastics club.

The sacrifice and training paid off. Shire received a scholarship from the University of Utah, which boasts of one of college
gymnastics' most successful programs. It was a dream come true.

Though all the circumstances and the situation promised that
Salt Lake City would be a perfect fit for Shire, it wasn't. She soon
realized that gymnastics "just was not fun anymore." She recalled her parents' declaration that "when the sport was no longer
enjoyable, they'd be done with it." So she gave it up.

Shire transferred to MU so she could be closer to her family.
She discovered, though, that she had three friends on the Mizzou
gymnastics team, and gradually she felt the sport pulling at her.
She met with coach Rob Drass and, "he lit that fire again," Shire
said. She cautiously decided to give gymnastics a second chance.

Shire was the Big 12 Newcomer of the Year in 2008. In 2009, she
was the league's Co-Gymnast of the Year and an All-American on

the vault. That only set the stage for her senior year.

In 2010, she won eleven all-around titles and was named the Big 12 Gymnast of the Year. She was ranked No. 1 in the nation in the all-around. More importantly for Mizzou athletic history, she led the team to its first-ever victory in the NCAA regional and a berth in the national NCAA competition.

In a sport that is largely one of perception, Drass said that in 2010 Missouri "earned our invitation in[to]" the club. This "is going to put us in a new league" — thanks in great part to Sarah Shire, who gave gymnastics a second chance.

"If I just had a second chance, I know I could make it work out." Ever said that? If only you could go back and tell your dad one last time you love him, take that job you passed up rather than relocate, or replace those angry shouts at your son with gentle encouragement. If only you had a second chance, a mulligan.

As the story of Jesus' encounter with the adulterous woman illustrates, with God you always get a second chance. No matter how many mistakes you make, God will never give up on you. Nothing you can do puts you beyond God's saving power. You always have a second chance because with God your future is not determined by your past or who you used to be. It is determined by your relationship with God through Jesus Christ.

God is ready and willing to give you a second chance — or a third chance or a fourth chance — if you will give him a chance.

They welcomed me with open arms.
    — Sarah Shire on the second chance MU gymnastics gave her

**You get a second chance with God
if you give him a chance.**

AS A RULE

Read Luke 5:27-32.

"Why do you eat and drink with tax collectors and 'sinners'?" (v. 30b)

The Tigers once used a tactic to win a football game that re-sulted in a change in the rules still in place today.

On Oct. 13, 1923, cold rain forced Mizzou and Iowa State into a punting duel with the two teams combining for thirty-five kicks. The punter for the Tigers was the legendary Don Faurot. (See devotions 37 and 44.) At one point, he mishandled the snap when trying to punt from close to the Tiger goal line. Center Clyde Smith, who went on to be a three-time All Pro, tried to take the blame, saying he had snapped the ball low. Faurot would have none of it. Wherever the fault lay, the result was a safety, and Iowa State won the game 2-0.

Three weeks later, a similar situation arose again. Heavy rain turned Kansas State's new field into a mudhole. The Tigers led 4-0 on a pair of safeties, and Faurot was backed up to his own goal line to punt with less than two minutes to play. The strategy was obvious: take a safety, especially when the rules in place let the team taking the safety retain possession at its own 30.

Head coach Gwinn Henry sent star halfback Art Bond into the game with instructions to give up the safety. Faurot refused. "But it's good strategy and the coach's orders," Bond said. "I know," the future head coach admitted, "but I lost a ball game giving up a safety. You do it." Bond did. He took the snap and stepped back to yield the safety. Missouri won 4-2.

The strategy was indeed sound, but the game's mavens realized the rules penalized the defense for excellent play. Missouri's tactic led to the rule change that even today requires a team giving up a safety to also give up possession.

Like college football players and coaches, you live by rules that others set up. Some lender determined the interest rate on your mortgage and your car loan. You work hours and shifts somebody else established. Someone else decided what day your garbage gets picked up and what school district your house is in.

Jesus encountered societal rules also, including a strict set of religious edicts that dictated what company he should keep, what people, in other words, were fit for him to socialize with, talk to, or share a meal with. Jesus ignored the rules, choosing love instead of mindless obedience and demonstrating his disdain for society's rules by mingling with the outcasts, the lowlifes, the poor, and the misfits.

You, too, have to choose when you find yourself in the presence of someone whom society deems undesirable. Will you choose the rules or love? Are you willing to be a rebel for love — as Jesus was for you?

I believe in rules. Sure I do. If there weren't any rules, how could you break them?
— Baseball Hall of Famer Leo Durocher

Society's rules dictate who is acceptable
and who is not, but love in the name of Jesus
knows no such distinctions.

A CHANGE OF PLANS

Read Genesis 18:20-33.

"The Lord said, 'If I find fifty righteous people in the city of Sodom, I will spare the whole place for their sake'" (v. 26).

The offense wasn't doing anything, so Mizzou quarterback Phil Snowden decided that what was needed was a drastic change of plans. He started making up plays in the huddle.

Frank Broyles spent one season — 1957 — as the head coach in Columbia before he bolted for Arkansas and a hall of fame career. Athletic director Don Faurot's insistence that Broyles limit his recruiting to athletes from Missouri apparently had much to do with the coach's abrupt departure.

The '57 team struggled on offense and went only 5-4-1, losing its last three games. Snowden, a sophomore, said Broyles "didn't dedicate a lot of time to offense. . . . We did not have many plays."

That shortcoming showed up in the Nebraska game of Oct. 26. As Snowden recalled it, "Nebraska wasn't a great team." The Corn-huskers, in fact, finished the season 1-9.

Nevertheless, they led MU 13-0 in the last half when Snowden decided it was time for a change no matter how bizarre it might seem. "I started calling plays in the huddle we didn't have," he recalled. "I was making up plays like 'sandlot,' telling [end] Russ Sloan and others, 'You do this and we are going to do this.'" (Sloan would earn honorable-mention All-American honors as a senior in 1959.)

It was certainly a major change in the approach to the offense, but it worked. The Tigers rallied, and fullback Hank Kuhlmann broke off what Snowden called "a pretty good run" that tied the game. The extra point gave Mizzou a stunning 14-13 win.

And what did the coaches have to say about Snowden's unauthorized changes? "Not a word was said by any coach," he said.

To be unable to adapt to changing circumstances to is stultify and die. It's true of animal life, of business and industry, of the military, of Missouri's football team, of you and your relationships, your job, and your finances.

Changing your plans regularly therefore is rather routine for you. But consider how remarkable it is that the God of the universe may change his mind about something. What could bring that about?

Prayer. Someone — whether it's an old nomad named Abraham or a 21st-century Missouri fan like you — talks to God, who listens and considers what is asked of him.

You may feel uncomfortable praying. Maybe you're reluctant and embarrassed; perhaps you feel you're not very good at it. But nobody majors in prayer at school, and as for being reluctant, what have you got to lose? Your answer may even be a change of plans on God's part. Such is the power of prayer.

I was worried about it. You don't do crazy things like calling your own plays.
— Phil Snowden, on the coaches' reaction to his changing the offense

Prayer is so powerful
that it may even change God's mind.

DANCING ANGELS

Read Luke 15:1-10.

"There is rejoicing in the presence of the angels of God over one sinner who repents" (v. 10).

What in the world was junior guard Zaire Taylor doing at 11 p.m. standing all alone on Norm Stewart Court in his uniform holding a basketball in his left hand and a sign with a marriage proposal from a fan in his right hand? Well, he was celebrating.

Head coach Mike Anderson established a rule that his Tiger players could spend no more than a few hours celebrating a win. Taylor, therefore, at midnight was to forget about what had just happened, so he was taking advantage of every second he had. This was Feb. 9, 2009, and Taylor had that night made the biggest shot of his young life in the biggest game of his young life.

Ineligible because of NCAA transfer rules, Taylor endured the lost season of 2007-08 sitting on the bench, unable to help his team. This was a new day, however. The Tigers entered the game of Feb. 9 against Kansas ranked 17th in the nation and in third place in the Big 12. Still, "everything is more important when the opponent is Kansas."

So they went out and scored 16 points in the first half and trailed 30-16. But "with a roaring crowd in their ears and the Tigers in their shorts," the Jayhawks started turning the ball over in the last half. MU tied the game at 60 and then had the last shot.

With time running out, Taylor put up a midrange jumper. The

TIGERS

shot hit the rim and bounced high in the air. Taylor said the ball seemed to hang above the basket before it dropped in slow motion through the hoop. Only 1.3 seconds were left. MU won 62-60.

A wild celebration ensued with Taylor at the heart of it. He was interviewed at midcourt by *ESPN*'s Holly Rowe but finally had to tell her, "I can't hear anything you're saying."

So there he was later that night, all alone on the court, celebrating one of the biggest wins in recent Mizzou basketball history.

You got that new job or that promotion. You just held your newborn child in your arms. Life has those grand moments that call for celebration. You may jump up and down and scream in a wild frenzy when Missouri wins or share a quiet, sedate candlelight dinner at home — but you celebrate.

Consider then a celebration that is beyond our imagining, one that fills every niche and corner of the very home of God and the angels. Imagine a celebration in Heaven, which has its grand moments too.

Those grand moments are touched off when someone comes to faith in Jesus. Heaven itself rings with the joyous sounds of the singing and dancing of the celebrating angels. Even God rejoices when just one person — you or someone you have introduced to Christ — turns to him. When you said "yes" to Christ, you made the angels dance. Most importantly of all, you made God smile.

I have to have a tooth pulled.
— Zaire Taylor on why he couldn't celebrate his newfound fame

God himself joins the angels in heavenly celebration when even a single person turns to him through faith in Jesus.

DAY 29

EASY DOES IT

Read John 6:53-66.

"[M]any of his disciples said, 'This is a hard teaching. Who can accept it?' . . . From this time many of his disciples turned back and no longer followed him" (vv. 60, 66).

Easy. That's what the game against Baylor was in the first quarter. After that, though, "what could have been an early runaway turned into a gut check" for the Tigers.

In the first fifteen minutes of the Nov. 1, 2008, game in Waco, Missouri quarterback Chase Daniel had a field day. He threw TD passes to Chase Coffman and Tommy Saunders and had the Tigers set to score again when the quarter ended. But on the first play of the second quarter, Baylor grabbed an interception to thwart the threat. Nothing was easy for Missouri after that.

After the teams swapped touchdowns in the second quarter, Baylor scored on its first two possessions of the last half. The "easy" game was tied at 21 heading into the final fifteen minutes.

MU reclaimed the lead with a second Daniel-to-Coffman TD toss, this one on the first play of the fourth quarter and covering 13 yards. Again, though, Baylor rallied to tie it, getting a touchdown with 9:54 to play.

With nothing coming easy for the Tigers, the Bears hauled in their second interception of the game and had a shot to take the lead for the first time. Its collective backs against the wall, the

TIGERS

Mizzou defense stood tough to force a punt.

The Tigers then took the hard way to claim the win, marching 75 yards in 13 plays. With 2:31 left, Jeff Wolfert booted a 34-yard field goal for a 31-28 lead. It held up when senior All-Big 12 linebacker Brock Christopher grabbed an interception of his own.

"It was a tremendous game," declared head coach Gary Pinkel. It certainly wasn't an easy one, though it looked like it at first.

Even if you're the Missouri Tigers, beating a quality opponent in football is never easy. Neither is following Jesus.

It's not just the often abstruse aspects of Jesus' teachings that test us mentally. It's that Jesus demands disruption in our lives. To take even a hesitant, tentative step toward following Jesus is to take a gigantic stride toward changing our lives – and change is never easy. In fact, we abhor it; all too often we choose to live in misery and unhappiness because it's familiar; the devil we know is better than the angel we don't.

Jesus also demands commitment. We who live in a secular, me-first age are to surrender our lives to him, to God's control. We are to think, act, live, and feel in a way totally counter to the prevailing philosophy of the world we temporarily call home. We are to keep our sights on the spiritual world, to offer up a life of service and sacrifice now in exchange for a future eternal reward.

None of that is easy. But neither was dying on a cross.

We found a way to win at the end when we had to.
— Gary Pinkel on the hard-fought win over Baylor in 2008

That which is easily accomplished in life
is rarely satisfying or rewarding;
this includes our following Jesus.

PROMISES, PROMISES

Read 2 Corinthians 1:16-20.

"No matter how many promises God has made, they are 'Yes' in Christ" (v. 20).

In the dressing room after his first MU team had seen its title hopes crushed by a sound whipping, an emotional Dan Devine made a promise that seemed totally far-fetched.

On Nov. 15, 1958, Devine took the Tigers into Norman with a shot at the Big Eight championship and the Orange Bowl. Oklahoma won easily 39-0 for its thirteenth straight league title.

After the game, the head coach surprised his players by jumping onto a training table. His voice trembling with emotion, Devine said, "I promise you seniors that two years from now when these sophomores return to Norman, we'll beat Oklahoma." It seemed a promise that would probably not be kept; Missouri had not won in Norman since 1936.

But two years later, the Tigers arrived in Norman undefeated and boasting the nation's top-ranked defense against the rush. Still, Oklahoma had not lost to a conference opponent at home in eighteen years. At first, the Sooners looked like that remarkable streak would roll on. On the fourth play of the game, Oklahoma broke a 70-yard touchdown run. It was the first rushing score the Tigers had yielded all season.

Before the half, though, the unruffled Tigers roared into a 24-12 lead. Oklahoma refused to fold, trailing only 24-19 as the fourth quarter began. On the first play, Norris Stevenson, son of a preacher man, took a pitchout and broke off a 60-yard touchdown run. He had had a 77-yard scoring run in the first half.

That did it. The Tigers added a field goal and another TD to post a 41-19 final.

In praising Stevenson's play, Bill Callahan wrote in the *St. Louis Post-Dispatch*, "The meek inherited the earth today." They also fulfilled a promise their head coach had made two seasons before.

When the polls came out, Missouri was ranked No. 1.

The promises you make don't say much about you while the promises you keep tell everything.

The promise to your daughter to be there for her softball game. To your son to help him with his math homework. To your parents to come see them soon. To your spouse to remain faithful until death parts you. And remember what you promised God?

You may carelessly throw promises around, but you can never outpromise God, who is downright profligate with his promises. For instance, he has promised to love you always, to forgive you no matter what you do, and to prepare a place for you with him in Heaven.

There's more good news in that God operates on this simple premise: Promises made are promises kept. You can rely absolutely on God's promises. The people to whom you make them should be able to rely just as surely on your promises.

A bold promise, indeed.
— *Writer Bob Broeg on Dan Devine's promise to beat Oklahoma*

**God keeps his promises just as those
who rely on you expect you to keep yours.**

FAMILY TRADITIONS

Read Mark 7:1-13.

"You have let go of the commands of God and are holding on to the traditions of men" (v. 8).

Seeking to halt mounting losses to Kansas, Missouri's coach began one of college football's most enduring traditions.

In 1911, when Chester L. Brewer took over as Missouri's athletic director and football coach, the program wasn't faring too badly overall — except in the ferocious rivalry with Kansas. The Tigers had defeated their archrival only four times in the first twenty meetings, including a 12-6 win in 1909.

Those first twenty games had all been played at neutral sites in Kansas City. In 1911, however, a new rule required that all college football games be played on campus, so the Jayhawks would come to Columbia and Rollins Field for the first time.

That provided Brewer with inspiration. He called on Mizzou alums from all over the country to come back home for the big game. The *Columbia Missourian* listed the names of those who planned to return. Alums attended dinners in their honor, fans organized pep rallies, and a parade and a bonfire contributed to the revelry. Some 1,600 people traveled to the game, and a crowd estimated at more than 9,000 packed Rollins Field.

With less than four minutes left in the game, MU captain Glen Shuck kicked a field goal that forged a 3-3- tie. In the final seconds, Billy Blees tackled a Kansas runner from behind to prevent a game-winning touchdown. Exuberant fans carried him off the field on their shoulders.

That 1911 game raised a tidy sum for the school's athletic facilities and turned the tide of the rivalry with Kansas. It also began what became known across the country as Homecoming.

You encounter traditions practically everywhere in your life. Your workplace may have casual Friday. Your family may have a particular way of decorating the Christmas tree, or it may gather to celebrate Easter at a certain family member's home.

Your church probably has traditions also. A particular type of music, for instance. Or how often you celebrate Communion. Or the order of worship.

Jesus knew all about religious tradition; after all, he grew up in the Church. He understood, though, the danger that lay in allowing tradition to become a religion in and of itself, and in his encounter with the Pharisees, Jesus rebuked them for just that.

Obviously, Jesus changed everything the world had ever known about faith, including the traditions that had gradually arisen to define the way the Jews of his day worshipped. Jesus declared that those who truly worship God do not do so by just observing various traditions, but rather by establishing a meaningful, deep-seated personal relationship with him.

Tradition in our faith life is useful only when it helps to draw us closer to God.

People love sports traditions because they unite an entire fan base.
— Bryan Sakakeeny, bleacherreport.com

Religious tradition has value only when it
serves to strengthen our relationship with God.

UNBELIEVABLE!

Read Hebrews 3:7-19.

*"See to it, brothers, that none of you has a sinful,
unbelieving heart that turns away from the living God"
(v. 12).*

The first time Ehren Earleywine saw Chelsea Thomas pitch in
high school, he figured his radar gun had malfunctioned, so unbelievable was what he found.

Earleywine took over the MU softball program in August 2006.
Through the 2014 season, he led the Tigers to postseason play
every year, including three berths in the College World Series.

In 2006, he received a video of a hard-throwing righthander
from Pleasantville, Iowa. It was Chelsea Thomas. Since the tape
came from her father and Earleywine knew that parents are often
prone to exaggeration, he was somewhat skeptical.

Nevertheless, he gave the tape a look but couldn't see much. It
"was grainy, you couldn't see her mechanics, and you couldn't tell
if the ball was moving," the coach said. But he could hear clearly
"this real loud thump every time [the ball] hit the catcher's mitt."

That sound led him to grab his radar gun and make a trip in
2008 to the cornfields of Iowa to scout Thomas. The first three
throws he saw from the 18-year-old left Earleywine bewildered.
They registered 70, 71, and 68 miles per hour; a typical college
softball pitch roars in at 60 to 65 mph. He politely excused himself
to fix what was apparently a defective radar gun.

After some shaking, tinkering, and twisting, he returned and told Thomas, "Go ahead and cut loose." She did. The next pitch was 73 mph. Now completely past his unbelief, Earleywine said, "I knew right then I had a chance to be a pretty good coach."

Thomas put together a quite unbelievable career at Mizzou from 2009-2013 with a year off for a medical redshirt. She is the winningest pitcher in school history (111) and MU's all-time strikeout leader (1,174). She was the first softball player in school history to be named a first-team All-America three times.

Much of what taxes the limits of our belief system has little effect on our lives. Maybe we don't believe in UFOs, honest politicians, or the viability of electric cars. A healthy dose of skepticism is a natural defense mechanism that helps protect us in a world that all too often has designs on taking advantage of us.

That's not the case, however, when Jesus and God are part of the mix. Quite unbelievably, we often hear people blithely assert they don't believe in God. Or brazenly declare they believe in God but don't believe Jesus was anything but a good man and a great teacher.

At this point, unbelief becomes dangerous because God doesn't fool around with scoffers. He locks them out of the Promised Land, which isn't a country in the Middle East but Heaven itself.

Given that scenario, it's downright unbelievable that anyone would not believe.

I'm banging this calibrator against a tree (to get it to vibrate).
— Ehren Earleywine on his reaction to Chelsea Thomas' first pitches

Perhaps nothing is as unbelievable as that some people insist on not believing in God or his son.

WHAT A SURPRISE!

Read 1 Thessalonians 5:1-11.

"But you, brothers, are not in darkness so that this day should surprise you like a thief" (v. 4).

Missouri coach Chauncey Simpson had a big — really big — surprise for the Kansas Jayhawks.

When head coach Don Faurot headed off to war after the 1942 season, Simpson, the first assistant, and Herb Bunker did what they could. Some 350 colleges gave up football until World War II was over, but the Big Six decided to play on.

Simpson had only three lettermen in 1943: Bull Reece, Jack Morton, and Bill Ekern. His team was largely 17-year-olds and young men the military wouldn't accept. Two games were cancelled because of travel restrictions. Still, the Tigers soldiered on, finishing a pretty fair 3-5.

Things were better in 1944, but not much. Simpson had a pair of stars in quarterback Paul Collins and running back Bill Dellastatious. The latter had received a medical discharge from the Navy. While visiting an aunt, he saw the Missouri campus and liked it, so he stayed rather than return to Clemson.

The '44 team also had a surprise star.

The squad went 3-5-2. As usual, the season ended with the Kansas game. At a rally the eve of the game, Simpson grinned and promised "a secret weapon" against the Jayhawks. It was sophomore tackle Jim Kekeris. Simpson moved his 273-lb. star lineman to fullback for the game.

"A tackle of unusual agility" who would make All-Big Six three times and second-team All-America in 1946, Kekeris was a "human battering ram [who bounced] through, over, and off" the Jawhawks all afternoon. He even ripped off a 32-yard gallop.

Behind their strong, surprisingly speedy surprise, the Tigers smashed their way to a 28-0 win.

Surprise birthday parties are a delight. And what's the fun of opening Christmas presents when we already know what's in them? Some surprises in life provide us with experiences that are both joyful and delightful.

Generally, though, we expend energy and resources to avoid most surprises and the impact they may have upon our lives. We may be surprised by the exact timing of a baby's arrival, but we nevertheless have the bags packed beforehand and the nursery all set for its occupant. Paul used this very image (v. 3) to describe the Day of the Lord, when Jesus will return to claim his own and establish his kingdom. We may be caught by surprise, but we must still be ready.

The consequences of being caught unprepared by a baby's insistence on being born are serious indeed. They pale, however, beside the eternal effects of not being ready when Jesus returns. We prepare ourselves just as Paul told us to (v. 8): We live in faith, hope, and love, ever on the alert for that great, promised day.

The big boy was just too hard for Kansas to stop.
— Chauncey Simpson on his surprise in 1944

The timing of Jesus' return will be a surprise;
the consequences should not be.

GOD'S CONQUERORS

Read John 16:19-33.

"In this world you will have trouble. But take heart! I have overcome the world" (v. 33b).

The Tigers simply had too much to overcome to even think about beating Southern Cal. Funny thing about that.

On Sept. 11, Missouri opened the 1976 football season against the eighth-ranked Trojans at the Coliseum in Los Angeles. The Tigers really didn't stand a chance in this one. The Trojans were loaded and were playing at home. Missouri starting quarterback Steve Pisarkiewicz was doubtful for the game after cutting a finger. The day before the game a tropical storm made sure it did indeed rain in Southern California, which meant the Tigers couldn't practice on Friday. The sloppy field worked in favor of Southern Cal's strong running game.

Nope. Missouri had too many obstacles in its way to win.

So in one of those games nobody could explain, MU went out and handed USC the most lopsided opening-game loss in the program's storied history. It was no fluke. The Tigers controlled the game from the start, scoring on their first possession. After USC tied it, Curtis Brown returned the ensuing kickoff 95 yards for a touchdown. Brown was the game's star, scoring three touchdowns with a fourth nullified by a penalty.

Missouri rolled to a 30-10 halftime lead, but the break didn't even slow the Tigers down. They came out and marched 81 yards

TIGERS

in the third quarter, scoring on a 24-yard reverse by Leo Lewis. The USC fans were streaming for the exits.

When the carnage finally ended, the Tigers had overcome what seemed like impossible odds to bury USC 46-25. Amid delirium in Columbia, a large group of students stayed up all night to meet the winners at the airport at 6 o'clock Sunday morning.

It was the only game Southern Cal lost all season.

We frequently hear inspiring stories of people who triumph by overcoming especially daunting obstacles such as the Tigers often face on the football field. Those barriers may be physical or mental disabilities or great personal tragedies or injustice. When we hear of them, we may well respond with a little prayer of thanksgiving that life has been kinder to us.

But all people of faith, no matter how drastic the obstacles they face, must ultimately overcome the same opponent: the Satan-infested world. Some do have it tougher than others, but we all must fight daily to remain confident and optimistic.

To merely survive from day to day is to give up by surrendering our trust in God's involvement in our daily life. To overcome, however, is to stand up to the world and fight its temptations that would erode the armor of our faith in Jesus Christ.

Today is a day for you to overcome by remaining faithful. The very hosts of Heaven wait to hail the conquering hero.

The eighth-ranked Trojans were loaded with talent, with a new coach, a wet field, and a vaunted running game.
— Donoho and O'Brien on what MU had to overcome vs. USC

**Life's difficulties provide us a chance
to experience the true joy of victory in Jesus.**

NO JOKE!

Read Romans 12:9-21.

"Do not be overcome by evil, but overcome evil with good" (v. 21).

During a recruiting visit to Brad Smith's home, the youngster's former youth football coach threatened to come after the visiting coach with a shotgun if he mistreated Smith. He was only joking, of course. Wasn't he?

The coach was Matt Eberflus, at the time an assistant football coach at Toledo. His boss was Gary Pinkel. For whatever reasons, the major colleges pretty much ignored Smith. "We still like this guy," Pinkel said. "This guy's good enough."

And he was. Smith became one of the greatest players in MU history. From 2002-05, he was a four-year starter, setting a number of school, conference, and collegiate records. He was the first player in Division 1-A history to pass for 8,000 yards and run for 4,000 yards in a career. He still holds the school records for career rushing yards (4,289), most points in a game (30), and most touchdowns in a game (5).

After the 2000 season, Eberflus and Pinkel had their sights set on making Smith a Toledo Rocket. Eberflus was honest with the family, informing them that the Toledo staff had other job prospects. (That would be Missouri.) He said that if they left Toledo, they would want Smith to follow them.

That's when Bob Ware, the Smith boys' former youth football

coach, spoke up. He told Eberflus, "I'm not going to have you all taking my boy all this far away and then mistreating him. I've seen that happen. . . . If it does, next time you see me I'll be coming in with my pump shotgun."

He was joking . . . maybe. When Eberflus made a subsequent recruiting visit, this time as a Missouri coach, he asked Smith's mother, "Where's the guy with the shotgun?"

Certainly the Bible is not a repository of side-splitting jokes, though some theologians have posited that Jesus' parables were actually sort of jokes for his time. Have you heard the one about the son who left his rich father and went to live with pigs?

No, the Gospel and its message of salvation and hope is serious stuff. Christians take it as such and well they should. Yet though many Christians might well vilify anyone who treats Jesus as a joke, those same persons themselves treat some aspects of Jesus' teachings as little more than gags not to be taken seriously.

Sexual purity, for instance. How outdated is that? And the idea of expecting answers to our prayers. What a silly notion! Surely Jesus was jesting when he spoke of tithing. How laughable is it to live performing selfless acts for others without getting the credit! And polls consistently reveal that about half of America's Christians don't believe in Hell. In other words, Jesus was joking.

No, he wasn't. If we think any of what Jesus taught us is a joke, then the joke's on us — and it's not very funny.

The part about the shotgun was a little out there. I may have smiled.
— Bob Ware on his 'joke' to Matt Eberflus

Jesus wasn't joking; if we really love him, then we will live in the manner he prescribed for us.

DAY 36

ON CALL

Read 1 Samuel 3:1-18.

"The Lord came and stood there, calling as at the other times, 'Samuel! Samuel!' Then Samuel said, 'Speak, for your servant is listening'" (v. 10).

Bench players, inexperienced freshmen, even an injured player — they all answered the call to help the Tigers pull off one of the most bizarre and exciting wins in their storied basketball history.

They were dubbed "the least impressive 5-1 team in history" when the Tigers took on ranked Illinois in St. Louis on Dec. 22, 1993. It didn't seem to matter much when senior forward Jevon Crudup fouled out late in the game since Illinois led by seven in the last minute. But senior guard Mark Atkins, Big Eight Player of the Year Melvin Booker, and senior guard-forward Lamont Frazier hit shots to tie the game and send it into overtime.

In the extra period, Atkins and junior forward Marlo Finner fouled out, but again it didn't seem to matter since Illinois led by five with 43 seconds left. Again, though, the Tigers pulled out a miraculous rally, this time using baskets by freshman forward Kelly Thames to forge an 88-88 tie and force a second OT.

MU got yet another miracle when an Illinois freshman missed two free throws with no time left. The game went into a third overtime, and by now head coach Norm Stewart was desperate for players. With four Tigers having fouled out, Stewart called on freshmen Jason Sutherland and Derek Grimm, who had seen

TIGERS

little playing time.

That didn't bother Sutherland, who immediately hit a three-pointer to start the overtime. MU never trailed again even though Booker, who set a school record with thirteen assists, fouled out. That forced Stewart to put Reggie Smith into the game. The senior guard hadn't played because he had a badly sprained ankle.

Frazier hit two free throws with 3.8 seconds left to nudge MU into a 108-107 win. An exhausted Stewart was just glad the game didn't last any longer; he was out of bodies to call on.

A team player is someone who does whatever the coach calls upon him to do for the good of the team. Something quite similar occurs when God places a specific call upon a Christian's life.

This is obviously much scarier than unexpectedly having to play in a close game as happened to some young and injured Tigers against Illinois. Many folks understand that answering God's call means going into the ministry, packing the family up, and moving halfway around the world to some place where folks have never heard of air conditioning, fried chicken, cell phones, or the Tigers. Zambia. The Philippines. Cleveland even.

Not for you, no thank you. And who can blame you?

But God usually calls folks to serve him where they are. In fact, God put you where you are right now, and he has a purpose in placing you there. Wherever you are, you are called to serve him.

We had the wounded in there. I guess the women and children would have been next.
— *Norm Stewart on the 1993 Illinois game*

**God calls you to serve him right now
right where he has put you, wherever that is.**

DAY 37

HOLLYWOOD ENDING

Read Luke 24:1-12.

"Why do you look for the living among the dead? He is not here; he has risen!" (vv. 5, 6a)

The final game of Don Faurot's coaching career at Missouri featured an ending so bizarre that Hollywood probably wouldn't make a movie of it because nobody would believe it.

Faurot has been called "one of the most innovative coaches in NCAA history." He won 101 games in his 19 seasons at the helm in Columbia, a school record broken by Gary Pinkel in the 2014 Cotton Bowl win over Oklahoma State. Faurot Field at Memorial Stadium is named after him; a 9-foot statue of him greets fans at the stadium's north entrance.

Before the 1956 season began, Faurot announced it would be his last one on the sidelines. The team did not play well, entering the final game against Kansas on Dec. 1 only 3-5-1. Kansas controlled most of the game and led 13-7 late in the fourth quarter. Starting quarterback Jim Hunter was out with a second-quarter injury, so Stub Clemensen and Dave Doane led the Tigers on one last charge.

With 3:12 left to play, end Larry Plumb caught a fourth-down touchdown pass — straight out of Hollywood — to knot the score at 13. Mizzou missed the PAT, though, and a tie looked certain.

But the Jayhawks considered a tie an upset and went for it on fourth down. Mizzou held at the KU 32 and then threw an interception. That heartbreak served to set up the Hollywood ending. From the 4, KU incredibly tried a reverse; tackle Chuck Mehrer read it perfectly and stuffed the play in the end zone for a safety with 39 seconds left. Missouri won 15-13.

His coaching career ending in true Hollywood fashion, Faurot went out in style. While their fans stormed the field, the Missouri players carted their legendary coach "off the field and into the sunset on their shoulders."

The world tells us that happy endings are for fairy tales and the movies, that reality is Cinderella dying in childbirth and her prince getting killed in a peasant uprising. But that's just another of the world's lies.

The truth is that Jesus Christ has been producing happy endings for almost two millennia. That's because in Jesus lies the power to change and to rescue a life no matter how desperate the situation. Jesus is the master at putting shattered lives back together, of healing broken hearts and broken relationships, of resurrecting lost dreams.

And as for living happily ever after — God really means it. The greatest Hollywood ending of them all was written on a Sunday morning centuries ago when Jesus left a tomb and death behind. With faith in Jesus, your life can have that same ending. You live with God in peace, joy, and love — forever. The End.

Don Faurot was *the University of Missouri.*
— *Warren Powers, Mizzou head football coach 1978-84*

**Hollywood's happy endings are products
of imagination; the happy endings Jesus
produces are real and are yours for the asking.**

DAY 38

BIG DEAL

Read Ephesians 3:1-13.

"His intent was that now, through the church, the
manifold wisdom of God should be made known" (v. 10).

What the Tigers did against Oklahoma on Oct. 23, 2010, was a
really big deal.

With five straight bowl appearances and Big 12 North championships in two of the last three seasons, the Missouri football
program had established itself as a consistent winner when the
2010 season began. Despite all those wins, however, the Tigers
had failed to claim a spot among college football's elite. That was
largely because they couldn't beat Oklahoma.

OU had been called "the bane of Mizzou's existence." Heading
into the 2010 game, Oklahoma had won 19 of the last 20 meetings,
including total beatdowns in the 2007 and '08 Big 12 title games.
Gary Pinkel put it plainly: "If you want to move your program
up a notch respect-wise, you have to win games like this."

He was referring to the 2010 contest, which seemed to present
Missouri with very limited opportunities to make a statement.
True, MU went into the game 6-0 and ranked 18th. On the other
hand, the dreaded Sooners were also 6-0 and were ranked No. 1.
The Tigers faced the heavy burden of history on two fronts: their
dismal record against Oklahoma and their failure ever to beat a
team ranked No. 1 in the nation.

That all changed on one glorious night in which "years of frus-

TIGERS

tration and anguish were dealt with" as the Tigers "at last showed [they] can play with college football's big boys."

On a jam-packed homecoming night at Faurot Field, Missouri beat OU 36-27. The Tigers rushed for 178 yards, and quarterback Blaine Gabbert threw for 308 more. "This isn't a national championship, but it's big for our football program," Pinkel said.

It was certainly a big deal for the fans, who stormed the field at game's end and immersed the players in a euphoric sea of gold.

Like Missouri's win over Oklahoma in 2010, "big deals" are important components of the unfolding of our lives. Our wedding, childbirth, a new job, a new house, big MU games, even a new car. In many ways, what we regard as a big deal is what shapes not only our lives but our character.

One of the most unfathomable anomalies of faith in America today is that while many people profess to be die-hard Christians, they disdain involvement with a local church. As Paul tells us, however, the Church is a very big deal to God; it is at the heart of his redemptive work; it is a vital part of his eternal purposes.

The Church is no accident of history. It isn't true that Jesus died and all he wound up with for his troubles was the stinking Church. It is no consolation prize.

Rather, the Church is the primary instrument through which God's plan of cosmic and eternal salvation is worked out. And it doesn't get any bigger than that.

Mizzou stepped up and showed how good it really is.
— Writer Tom Timmerman on the big-deal win over OU in 2010

To disdain church involvement is to assert that God doesn't know what he's doing.

GREAT EXPECTATIONS

Read John 1:43-51.

"'Nazareth! Can anything good come from there?'
Nathanael asked" (v. 46).

The Tigers expected to get 2 yards and a first down on the play. Instead, they got a championship.

On Nov. 30, 2013, Missouri's football team took the field for the most pressure-packed game in the program's recent history. The opposition was the 19th-ranked Texas A&M Aggies, led by their Heisman-Trophy quarterback, Johnny Manziel. Riding on the game's outcome was the championship of the SEC's East Division and a berth in the league's title game. If the 5th-ranked Tigers won, they were champs; if they lost, they were not. It was simple.

The game was not. For the first time the entire season, MU trailed at halftime. The Tigers came out in the third quarter with a vengeance, quickly scoring twice to take a 21-14 lead. But with 10:43 to go, the Aggies tied the game. They would do nothing else as the Mizzou defense held them to 1 yard on nine plays over their final three drives. That gave the offense the chance to win the game and the title with a score. It did.

After some punts, the Tigers started from their 34 as the clock rolled down to under five minutes. Senior running back Henry Josey got 4 yards, and senior quarterback James Franklin got 5. That set up a crucial third-and-one, and offensive coordinator Josh Henson called on Josey for a play he expected to gain 2 yards.

TIGERS

That would pick up the first down and keep the clock moving.

Josey got much more. He took Franklin's handoff, "hit the line, cut back to his right, hurled over an ankle tackle and broke into the open field." Nobody would catch him. Senior left tackle Justin Britt thought about it. "I was going down to chase him," he said, "but I quickly remembered that's not going to happen."

Fifty-seven yards downfield, Josey was in the end zone, and Mizzou had a 28-21 win and a championship nobody expected.

The blind date your friend promised would look like Brad Pitt or Jennifer Aniston but instead bore a startling resemblance to the bride of Frankenstein or Cousin Itt. Your vacation that went downhill after the lost luggage. Often your expectations are raised only to be dashed. Sometimes it's best not to get your hopes up; then at least you have the possibility of being surprised.

Worst of all, perhaps, is when you realize that you are the one not meeting others' expectations. The fact is, though, that you aren't here to live up to what others think of you. Jesus didn't; in part, that's why they killed him. But he did meet God's expectations for his life, which was all that really mattered.

Because God's kingdom is so great, God does have great expectations for any who would enter, and you should not take them lightly. What the world expects from you is of no importance; what God expects from you is paramount.

A big hole opened up and I took it.
— Henry Josey on the run on which he expected to gain a first down

You have little if anything to gain from meeting the world's expectations of you; you have all of eternity to gain from meeting God's.

DAY 40

AMAZING!

Read: Luke 4:31-36.

"All the people were amazed and said to each other, 'What is this teaching? With authority and power he gives orders to evil spirits and they come out!'" (v. 36)

More amazing than the Mets!" So crowed a sportswriter over Missouri's miraculous win over Air Force.

On Sept. 20, 1969, the Falcons from the Academy had apparently pulled out a last-gasp win in the season opener. Missouri led 16-10 with only 1:27 to play when Air Force stunned the home crowd with a 57-yard bomb on fourth-and-21 down to the Tiger 23. Two plays later with only 32 ticks on the clock, another pass netted a touchdown. The extra point finished off an amazing Air Force comeback for a 17-16 win.

Offensive tackle Mike Carroll admitted he "was a little down when we got the ball again with so little time left." Then he found a little divine inspiration. "I remembered a verse from Matthew: 'Oh men of little faith.'"

Abiding faith was indeed required by the Missouri fans when junior college transfer quarterback Terry McMillan led the Tigers onto the field at their 24. Everyone expected the obvious: a deep throw to speedy wide receiver Mel Gray. The future MU hall-of-famer would hold the school record for career receiving yards for twenty years. He was also a five-time Big Eight Conference sprint champion.

TIGERS

When Gray drew double coverage, McMillan looked to sophomore wide receiver John Henley. Amazingly, the two connected on a 56-yard bomb down to the Air Force 20. Mizzou worked the clock down to 11 seconds before Henry Brown tied a conference record with his fourth field goal of the game.

The amazing final score of 19-17 was on the board.

The word *amazing* defines the limits of what you believe to be plausible or usual. The Grand Canyon, the birth of your children, those last-second Tiger wins — they're amazing! You've never seen anything like that before!

Some people in Galilee felt the same way when they encountered Jesus. Jesus amazed them with the authority of his teaching, and he wowed them with his power over spirit beings. People everywhere just couldn't quit talking about him.

It would have been amazing had they not been amazed. They were, after all, witnesses to the most amazing spectacle in the history of the world: God himself was right there among them walking, talking, teaching, preaching, and healing.

Their amazement should be a part of your life too because Jesus still lives. The almighty and omnipotent God of the universe seeks to spend time with you every day – because he loves you. Amazing!

More amazing than the Mets, more discouraging than a flunked final, more beautiful than Purple Mountain's Majesty and Raquel Welch.
– Sportswriter Doug Grow on MU's amazing win over Air Force in '69

Everything about God is amazing,
but perhaps most amazing of all is that
he loves us and desires our company.

DAY 41

DOWNRIGHT CRAZY

Read Luke 13:31-35.

"Some Pharisees came to Jesus and said to him, 'Leave this place and go somewhere else. Herod wants to kill you.' He replied, 'Go tell that fox . . . I must keep going today and tomorrow and the next day'" (vv. 31-33).

Mark Ellis wasn't one of the crazies anymore, and he missed it. So he switched sports and won a national championship.

Ellis started wrestling when he was 6 years old and was good enough to receive a scholarship offer from Missouri. He dreamed, however, "of donning shoulder pads instead of a singlet" at MU. So he turned down the free ride wrestling offered and walked onto the football team.

It didn't go well. Ellis needed less than two weeks to appreciate that football wasn't right for him. His decision was made easier by the football players' perception of college wrestlers. He had always thought that football players were the hardest workers, but "some of the football players were talking about how crazy the wrestlers were because of how hard they train."

When he heard those comments, Ellis realized that wrestlers were indeed crazy about their training, and he missed that.

So he hiked to the offices of MU wrestling coach Brian Smith and accepted the scholarship that was still available. Ellis started training, but the change to college wrestling was such a challenge for him that he seriously considered leaving school.

TIGERS

That's when assistant coach Ben Askren, MU's first national-champion wrestler, moved in as Ellis' mentor and helped change the young wrestler's life. A man of deep Christian faith, Ellis said he saw how Askren lived, how much he enjoyed life, "and how you could do all that and still train and work hard. I'm incredibly lucky God put people like him in my path."

Wrestling as a heavyweight in 2009, his junior season, Ellis won the individual national title as the Tigers won their third national crown. He is now indelibly branded as one of Mizzou's "wrestling crazies," which is what he wanted in the first place.

What some see as crazy often is shrewd instead. Like the time you went into business for yourself or when you decided to go back to school. Maybe it was when you fixed up that old house. Or when you bought that new company's stock.

You know a good thing when you see it but are also shrewd enough to spot something that's downright crazy. Jesus was that way too. He knew that his entering Jerusalem was in complete defiance of all apparent reason and logic since a whole bunch of folks who wanted to kill him were waiting for him there.

Nevertheless, he went because he also knew that when the great drama had played out he would defeat not only his personal enemies but the most fearsome enemy of all: death itself.

It was, after all, a shrewd move that provided the way to your salvation.

Man, I'm one of those crazies. I miss that.
— Mark Ellis on why he left football for wrestling

It's so good it sounds crazy — but it's not: through faith in Jesus, you can have eternal life with God.

BEST FRIENDS

Read Ecclesiastes 4:9-12.

"If one falls down, his friend can help him up. But pity the man who falls and has no one to help him up!" (v. 10)

John Kadlec agreed to help out a friend for one day. What resulted was a 16-year career.

The man affectionately and widely known as "Mr. Mizzou" started his 50+ years of association with MU athletics in 1948 as a sophomore guard. He had played for St. Louis University as a freshman and had enjoyed a rather unforgettable debut. With no training table, Kadlec "naively had polished off at home before the night game a meal of sauerkraut and spare ribs." After a little bit of exertion and contact, he came out of the game vomiting with "the granddaddy of upset stomachs."

Kadlec went on to an All-Big Seven Conference career at MU. After he graduated, he stayed on as a graduate assistant, freshman coach, and assistant coach.

When Kadlec left coaching, he went to K-State as an administrator before coming back home to Columbia in 1986 to head up fundraising efforts. A fixture in the athletic department, he was inducted into the MU Athletics Hall of Fame in 1996. The grass practice fields were named in his honor in 2005.

Two days before the beginning of the 1995 football season, the color commentator spot on the MU radio network unexpectedly came open. Athletic Director Joe Castiglione asked Kadlec to fill the spot for the first game as a special favor. "I didn't really want to," Kadlec said. "I told him I'd think about it, figuring he'd maybe move on to somebody else."

But Castiglione didn't. When he came back an hour later, Kadlec realized the AD wasn't going to take no for an answer, so he said he'd work the one game. After that game, Castiglione told him, "I've got the guy who will do it. It's you." Kadlec agreed to do it for one year. That one year lasted through the 2010 season, after which Kadlec, who had expected to work only one game as a favor to a friend, finally turned his microphone off for good.

Lend him your car or some money. Provide tea, sympathy, and comfort when she's down. What wouldn't you do for a friend?

We are wired for friendship. Our psyche drives us to seek both the superficial company of others that casual acquaintance provides and the more meaningful intimacy that true friendship furnishes. We are perhaps at our noblest when we selflessly help a friend.

So if we wouldn't think of turning our back on our friends, why would we not be the truest, most faithful friend of all by sharing with them the gospel of Jesus Christ? Without thinking, we give a friend a ride, but we know someone for years and don't do what we can to save her from eternal damnation. Apparently, we are quite willing to spend all of eternity separated from our friends. What kind of lousy friend is that?

I said I'd do it for one game to help out a friend.
— John Kadlec on how he wound up behind a microphone

**A true friend introduces a friend
to his friend Jesus.**

DAY 43

ULTIMATE MAKEOVER

Read 2 Corinthians 5:11-21.

"If anyone is in Christ, he is a new creation; the old has gone, the new has come!" (v. 17)

Max Copeland figured he had to make some changes to get a shot at the NFL, so the Missouri offensive lineman made himself over — into a fullback.

Copeland was called "a great story of perseverance and determination," who turned down a scholarship offer from Montana to walk on at Missouri. Before the start of his junior season in 2012, he was awarded a scholarship and started at guard his last two seasons in Columbia. He was regarded "as the fringiest of fringe NFL prospects" despite his strong senior season.

And then Copeland had a dream, a vision of his playing fullback. "It felt right. It felt fun," he said. He checked in with his mother for affirmation. She agreed it would be fun, something they could talk about ten years down the road whether he made an NFL roster or not.

So Copeland set out to make himself over — secretly. Only Pat Ivey, a former strength coach who runs MU's player development program, and the players he trained with — including his close friend, linebacker Andrew Wilson — knew what he was up to.

Copeland cut his caloric intake and hit the gym for eight hours a day. "I would work until I puked and then keep working," he said. In a little less than two months he lost 50 pounds of fat.

When Wilson saw him in March 2014 after being away for six weeks, he was astounded. "I was like, 'What the heck happened?'" he said. "I called him thin. He doesn't like that."

Copeland also approached MU quarterback James Franklin about throwing to him and teaching him some routes and the finer points of catching a pass. Franklin responded with a hearty and immediate "yes." "What a loyal dude," Copeland said.

So at Missouri's Pro Day on March 20, 2014, Max Copeland the former guard weighed in at 268 pounds, ran routes, and caught passes for some NFL scouts.

Ever considered a makeover? TV shows show us how changes in clothes, hair, and makeup and some weight loss can radically alter the way a person looks. But these changes are only skin deep. Even with a makeover, the real you — the person inside — remains unchanged. How can you make over that part of you?

By giving your heart and soul to Jesus — just as you give up your hair to the makeover stylist. You won't look any different; you won't dance any better; you won't suddenly start talking smarter. The change is on the inside where you are brand new because the model for all you think and feel is now Jesus. He is the one you care about pleasing.

Made over by Jesus, you realize that gaining his good opinion — not the world's — is all that really matters. And he isn't the least interested in how you look but how you act.

I'm always changing faces, man. I'm always trying to be unrecognizable.
— Max Copeland on making himself over into a fullback

**Jesus is the ultimate makeover artist; he can make
you over without changing the way you look.**

SOMETHING NEW

Read Ephesians 4:17-24.

*"You were taught . . . to put off your old self . . . and
to put on the new self, created to be like God in true
righteousness and holiness" (vv. 22, 24).*

The Tigers of 1941 came within a touchdown of the national
championship in large part because of something new their head
coach introduced to collegiate football that season.

Don Faurot is a University of Missouri legend. From 1922-24,
he lettered at Mizzou in football, baseball, and basketball and
then returned to his alma mater in 1935 as the head football coach.
He led the Tigers for nineteen seasons and set a school record for
wins. He served as the Missouri athletic director from 1935-42
and from 1946-66. He was the fifth person inducted into the State
of Missouri Sports Hall of Fame in 1953 and was inducted into the
College Football Hall of Fame in 1961.

In 1941, Faurot cemented his place in college football history
when he introduced the Split T formation. His Tigers had ridden
the arm of Paul Christman to twenty wins and a Big Six championship from 1938-40. With his graduation, the team's strength
became its running backs (Bob Steuber, Harry Ice, and Maurice
Wade) and its offensive line with All-American center Darold
Jenkins, All-Big Six guard Mike Fitzgerald, and tackle Bob Jeffries.

So Faurot tinkered with a way to open up the running game.
He widened the spacing among the offensive linemen, producing

more lanes to run through. The result was the birth of option football, leading to derivatives such as the Wishbone and the Veer.

Faurot used the newfangled formation for one possession in the '41 season opener against Ohio State. The result was a touchdown, but Missouri lost 12-7. After that, he went all in with the Split T, and Missouri rolled through the rest of the schedule. The Tigers finished 8-1, wound up ranked seventh in the country, and led the nation in rushing. One more possession with that new formation may well have meant the national title.

New things in our lives often have a life-changing effect. A new spouse. A new baby. A new job. Even something as mundane as a new television set or lawn mower jolts us with change.

While new experiences, new people, and new toys may make our lives new, they can't make new lives for us. Inside, where it counts – down in the deepest recesses of our soul – we're still the same, no matter how desperately we may wish to change.

An inner restlessness drives us to seek escape from a life that is a monotonous routine. Such a mundane existence just isn't good enough for someone who is a child of God; it can't even be called living. We want more out of life; something's got to change.

The only hope for a new life lies in becoming a brand new man or woman. And that is possible only through Jesus Christ, he who can make all things new again.

Don Faurot made the only significant change in offensive football in seventy-five years. Almost everything is an offshoot of his old Split T.
— Dan Devine in 1995

A brand new you with the promise of a life worth living is waiting in Jesus Christ.

DAY 45

FAMILY TIES

Read Mark 3:31-35.

"[Jesus] said, 'Here are my mother and my brothers! Whoever does God's will is my brother and sister and mother'" (vv. 34-35).

Most Missouri athletes have a family cheering them on and supporting them. Caitlyn Vann had two.

Vann was one of the most productive defensive players in MU volleyball history. A starting libero for three years (A libero is a defensive specialist.), she was a star as a senior on the 2010 squad that advanced to the Sweet 16. She set the school record for digs in a season and is fourth all-time in digs in Big 12 history.

Vann had plenty of support at Mizzou what with two families and her faith. About those two families. When Vann was born, her 19-year-old mother was a college softball player and felt her daughter deserved a more stable environment than she could provide. "I'm not your crackhead mom," she said. So she made the difficult decision to put her daughter up for adoption.

A husband-and-wife team of professors at Ball State adopted Caitlyn. "I couldn't have asked for more from my parents," Caitlyn said. "They're amazing." The adoption was closed, but Caitlyn's mother sent constant updates to the adoption agency, so the birth mother could know Caitlyn was doing well.

When she was 9, Caitlyn's life took a twist. Her birth mother's sister was assigned to her class at a Ball State laboratory school

TIGERS

and recognized her niece from pictures. Caitlyn's curiosity about her birth family was aroused, and her adoptive parents agreed it would be good for her to contact her birth mother. They corresponded and then met for the first time when Caitlyn was in the eighth grade. Thus, she wound up with a second family, growing close to her birth mother and her half-siblings.

She also found faith. Her adoptive parents are atheists, but her birth mother is a devout Christian. Her influence led Caitlyn to Christ. She played at Mizzou with two tattoos relating to God.

Some wit said families are like fudge, mostly sweet with a few nuts. You can probably call the names of your sweetest relatives, whom you cherish, and of the nutty ones too, whom you mostly try to avoid at a family reunion.

Like it or not, you have a family, and that's God's doing. God cherishes the family so much that he chose to live in one as a son, a brother, and a cousin.

One of Jesus' more radical actions was to redefine the family. No longer is it a single household of blood relatives or even a clan or a tribe. Jesus' family is the result not of an accident of birth but rather of a conscious choice. All those who do God's will are members of Jesus' family.

What a startling and downright wonderful thought! You have family members out there you don't even know who stand ready to love you just because you're part of God's family.

God has played a major role in my life.
— Caitlyn Vann on the faith she received from her birth family

**For followers of Jesus, family comes not
from a shared ancestry but from a shared faith.**

BEING DIFFERENT

Read Daniel 3.

*"We want you to know, O king, that we will not serve
your gods or worship the image of gold you have set up"
(v. 18).*

From a ride on a fire truck to practice in a horse stable, MU football in the early '60's was different from what it is today.

Celebrations were different back then. After the Tigers waxed Oklahoma 41-19, (See Devotion No. 30.), the Associated Press voted them No. 1 in the nation. All-American end Conrad Hitchler remembered that when the team arrived home after the win, "A fire truck met us at the airport and there was a parade through town." The impromptu celebration wound its way to Memorial Union, "and everyone got up and said a few words."

During a snowy December day as the 1960 team prepared for the Orange Bowl, Dan Devine took his boys to the Stephens College horse stable to practice out of the bad weather. The result was a great session. Hitchler called it "probably the best thing that could have happened. The guys were *killing* each other because all the Stephens girls were standing around the arena watching."

Recruiting was different back then, too. Running back and kicker Bill Tobin didn't have any splashy TV show to announce his decision. He had decided on Iowa, but one day when his dad and he were in the barn milking cows, Tobin Senior said, "We are *Missouri* people, and we pay *Missouri* taxes. I think it would be a

TIGERS

good idea if you went to Missouri." Thus was the decision made.

The 1961 squad had to reach a different decision. They finished 7-2-1 and received an invitation to the Bluebonnet Bowl. Devine let the players vote on it, which would be unheard of today. Even more of unheard of is that the players decided not to go. "I don't think the coaches wanted us to go or they wouldn't have let us vote," explained defensive back Carl Crawford.

College football was just different back then.

While we live in a secular society that constantly pressures us to conform to its principles and values, we serve a risen Christ who calls us to be different. Therein lies the great conflict of the Christian life in contemporary America.

But how many of us really consider that even in our secular society we struggle to conform? We are all geeks in a sense. We can never truly conform because we were not created by God to live in such a sin-filled world in the first place. Thus, when Christ calls us to be different by following and espousing Christian beliefs, principles, and practices, he is summoning us to the lifestyle we were born for.

The most important step in being different for Jesus is realizing and admitting what we really are: We are children of God; we are Christians. Only secondarily are we citizens of a secular world. That world both scorns and disdains us for being different; Jesus both praises and loves us for it.

The season was long, and it was kind of a no-name bowl.
— Carl Crawford on the decision not to play in the Bluebonnet Bowl

**The lifestyle Jesus calls us to is different from that
of the world, but it is the way we were born to live.**

DAY 47

THANKS A LOT

Read 1 Thessalonians 5:12-28.

*"[G]ive thanks in all circumstances, for this is God's will
for you in Christ Jesus" (v. 18).*

Before he even completed the downright miraculous play that
rescued Missouri from a disastrous defeat, T.J. Moe was giving
thanks to God.

The 2-0 Tigers were two-touchdown favorites over San Diego
State on Sept. 18, 2010. The Aztecs had lost 22 straight games to
BCS conference opponents, but on this particular night, the cup-
cake was laced with arsenic. As writer Joe Walljasper put it, "The
Tigers' delusions of grandeur gave way to the desperate hope that
somehow, some way, . . . they could just squeak this one out."

It sure didn't look like they would. With only 1:22 to play, the
Tigers trailed 24-20, sat on their own 12, and had only one timeout
to play with. In the huddle, slot receiver Moe shook quarterback
Blaine Gabbert's hand, looked him in the eye, and said, "All right,
Blaine, it's time to be great." What resulted is now part of MU lore.

On the first play, Gabbert found junior wide receiver Jerrell
Jackson for 20 yards. Then came the play that "changed the for-
tunes of Missouri's young season in one flash." At the line of
scrimmage, Gabbert changed the play. He called for Jackson to
run a deep fade down the left sideline and Moe to cut inside on a
6-yard out pattern.

Gabbert got the ball to Moe. "I caught the ball, turned around

TIGERS

and saw him and just stopped," Moe said. "Him" was an Aztec defender, and Moe juked him off his feet. After that, Moe was thinking about getting out of bounds.

But Jackson peeled back and clobbered a pair of defenders chasing Moe. They collided, clearing a lane for the sophomore to play the hero by racing 68 yards for a touchdown.

Around the 20-yard line, Moe called on Jesus and said, "Thanks for giving me this ability and saving me because I didn't play well in the first half."

MU won 27-24 as "pure elation erased embarrassment."

Thank you, Lord, for my cancer. Thank you, Lord, for my unemployment. Thank you, Lord, that my children are in trouble with the law. Is this what the Bible means when it tells us to always be thankful?

Of course not. Being a man of reasonably good sense, Paul didn't tell us to give thanks for everything that happens to us, but to give thanks to God even when bad things occur. The joy we know in our soul through Jesus, the prayers we offer to God, and the gratitude we feel for the blessings that are in our lives even in the midst of distress — these don't change no matter what.

Failure to thank God implies that we believe we alone are responsible for the good things in our lives. Such arrogance relegates God to the fringes of our lives. Constant gratitude keeps God right where he belongs in our lives: at the heart and soul.

The more you give thanks, the more you find things to be thankful for.
— Weightlifter Bob Hoffman

No matter what, we can always be thankful
for God's presence in our lives.

HERO WORSHIP

Read 1 Samuel 16:1-13.

"Do not consider his appearance or his height, for . . . the
Lord does not look at the things man looks at. . . . The
Lord looks at the heart" (v. 7).

The Tigers appeared headed for a last-minute, heartbreaking loss to Kansas — until the unlikeliest hero of all showed up.

After coming close to upsetting powerhouse Maryland in the season opener, the '52 football team beat Oklahoma A&M and then lost three straight games. That 1-4 start led head coach Don Faurot to close the practice gates at Rollins Field and hold election of team captains. Senior guard Bob Castle and junior defensive back Bob Schoonmaker received the honors.

"We really came back," Schoonmaker said. The team recovered to win three straight before a loss to Oklahoma set up the finale against a favored 7-2 Kansas team.

Fullback Bill Rowekamp broke an 82-yard run, and running back Nick Carras scored from the 3, but Kansas led 19-14 in the fourth quarter. Sophomore end Jack Hurley blocked a pass and then pulled it down for an interception at the Jayhawk 13. That set up a touchdown run on a busted play by quarterback Tony Scardino, and Missouri had a 20-19 lead.

But Kansas still had six minutes to save itself. With time running out, the Jayhawks faced third and 3 at the Tiger 15. The Tigers desperately needed a hero. They got one.

TIGERS

On the field was Bill Fessler, the team's senior punter. He had not played a down on defense all season, but injuries had thinned the secondary until he was the only player left. Kansas hit a pass over the middle for an apparent touchdown, but Fessler blasted the receiver with such a crushing tackle that he knocked himself out. But he also knocked the ball loose.

When Kansas missed a field goal, Missouri's unlikely hero had preserved a 20-19 Tiger upset.

On the field or the court, a hero is someone like Bill Fessler who makes a big play to save or win a game. In general, a hero is thought of as someone who performs brave and dangerous feats that save or protect someone's life. You figure you're excluded.

But ask your son about that when you show him how to bait a hook or throw a football, or your daughter when you show up for her honors night at school. Look into the eyes of those Little Leaguers you help coach.

Ask God about heroism when you're steady in your faith. For God, a hero is a person with the heart of a servant. And if a hero is a servant who acts to save other's lives, then the greatest hero of all is Jesus Christ.

God seeks heroes today, those who will proclaim the name of their hero — Jesus — proudly and boldly, no matter how others may scoff or ridicule. God knows heroes when he sees them — by what's in their hearts.

Heroes and cowards feel exactly the same fear; heroes just act differently.
— Boxing trainer Cus D'Amato

**God's heroes are those who remain steady
in their faith while serving others.**

GOOD ADVICE

Read Isaiah 8:11-9:7.

"And he will be called Wonderful Counselor" (v. 9:6b).

Missouri's head football coach took the advice he got from his son. The result was an All-American player.

Al Onofrio headed up the Missouri program for seven seasons, from 1971-77. Overall, he spent twenty years on the Mizzou football coaching staff. He was inducted into the MU Athletics Hall of Fame in 1993.

In the late 1960s, John Moseley was making headlines on the football field at Columbia's Hickman High School. Despite all his press clippings, he was considered too small for big-time ball. He was described as a "grinning squirt from around town" and a "mighty mite." The sports editor of the *El Paso Times* said he was "no more than knee-high to a powder keg." The Missouri coaches took a quick glance Moseley's way and moved on.

Someone who knew Moseley well, though, spoke up on his behalf. Eddie Onofrio, the coach's son and one of Moseley's high school teammates, just couldn't keep quiet. Since he had an inside with the head coach, he took it, urging the head Tiger to give Moseley a serious look.

Onofrio took his son's advice. When Moseley walked on, he got a shot at playing. The result was the only player in Missouri football history to go from walk-on to All-America (1973). A daring kick return man described as "one of the most exciting players

TIGERS

ever to play at MU," Moseley averaged 13.3 yards per punt return for his career, still the school record. As a senior, he led the Big Eight in both yards per punt return and yards per kickoff return.

Helped along by some timely advice his head coach took, John Moseley was an MU star, a Hall of Fame inductee in 1995.

Like Al Onofrio, we all need a little advice now and then. More often than not, we turn to professional counselors, who are all over the place. Marriage counselors, grief counselors, guidance counselors in our schools, rehabilitation counselors, all sorts of mental health and addiction counselors — We even have pet counselors. No matter what our situation or problem, we can find plenty of advice for the taking.

The problem, of course, is that we find advice easy to offer but hard to swallow. We also have a rueful tendency to solicit the wrong source for advice, seeking counsel that doesn't really solve our problem but that instead enables us to continue with it.

Our need for outside advice, for an independent perspective on our situation, is actually God-given. God serves many functions in our lives, but one role clearly delineated in his Word is that of Counselor. Jesus himself is described as the "Wonderful Counselor." All the advice we need in our lives is right there for the asking; we don't even have to pay for it except with our faith. God is always there for us: to listen, to lead, and to guide.

Gee, Dad, you've just got to take a good look at John [Moseley].
— Eddie Onofrio to Al

**We all need and seek advice in our lives,
but the ultimate and most wonderful counselor
is of divine and not human origin.**

JINXED

Read Jonah 1.

"Tell us, who is responsible for making all this trouble for us? What did you do?" (v. 8a)

Tim Jamieson was convinced his team had been the victim of a jinx, so he took care of that: no hats and T-shirts, please.

Jamieson became Missouri's head baseball coach when Gene McArtor retired after the 1994 season. Over the years, Jameison had led the Tigers into the championship game of the Big 12 Tournament three times: 2004, 2009, and 2011. Each time the team had held leads but had lost.

They weren't the favorites among the tournament field in 2012 after an up-and-down season. But they got a strong start from sophomore lefty Rob Zastryzny in the opening game and beat Texas 5-0. The win was Jamieson's 600th as the Mizzou boss.

The Tigers then pulled off an impressive 5-3 win over second-seeded Texas A&M behind strong pitching from starter Blake Holovach and Jeff Emens and what was called "a Ruthian homer" from senior outfielder Blake Brown.

After run-ruling Kansas 12-2, Jamieson's Tigers were back in the championship game for the fourth time. That set the veteran head coach to recalling those other title contests. He remembered something each loss had in common: the presence of officials from the league in the dugout waiting to pass out championship hats and T-shirts to the winners.

TIGERS

That was it! Those hats and T-shirts obviously had jinxed the Tigers. So Jamieson politely made a request of the league. He asked, "Please don't jinx us with the hat and T-shirt people again."

This time they stayed away and — sure enough — Missouri won the championship by edging Oklahoma in an 8-7 thriller.

Baseball players and coaches — including Tim Jamieson — are widely known to be a superstitious bunch, but hexes and jinxes don't really determine the outcome of a game. Missouri beat OU in 2012 because the Tigers scored one more run than the Sooners did, not because the dugout lacked hats and T-shirts.

Some people do feel, however, that they exist under a dark and rainy cloud. Nothing goes right; all their dreams collapse around them; they seem to constantly bring about misery on themselves and also on the ones around them. Why? Is it really a hex, a jinx?

Nonsense. The Bible provides us an excellent example in Jonah. The sailors on the boat with the reluctant prophet believed him to be a hex and the source of their bad luck. Jonah's life was a mess, but it had nothing to do with any jinx. His life was in shambles because he was disobeying God.

Take a careful look at people you know whose lives are in shambles, including some who profess to believe in God. The key to life lies not in belief alone; the responsibility of the believer is to obey God. Problems lie not in hexes but in disobedience.

I don't believe in a jinx or a hex. Winning depends on how well you block and tackle.

— Auburn coaching legend Shug Jordan

**Hexes don't cause us trouble,
but disobedience to God sure does.**

PLAN AHEAD

Read Psalm 33:1-15.

"The plans of the Lord stand firm forever, the purposes of his heart through all generations" (v. 11).

For T.J. Moe, The Plan was about football. There was no place in it for girls.

Longtime Missouri assistant coach Andy Hill said in 2012 that he could think of only three MU football players of whom it could be asserted they not only loved football, they lived it: running back Brock Olivo, defensive end Justin Smith, and Moe.

A wide receiver, Moe wrapped up his Mizzou career in 2012 with 188 catches, the fifth-highest total in school history. Three times he earned first-team all-conference academic honors.

"If you prioritize behind his faith and his family, football is it," Hill said of Moe. Moe's single-minded approach to football was in accordance with The Plan, which aimed to make him the best possible football player and the best teammate he could be.

Young T.J. had excelled at football since he was 7 and was in the seventh grade when his dad, Dave, drew up The Plan. Its heart and soul was endless preparation. Each morning, for instance, Dave dropped T.J. off at school at 5:30 a.m. so he could lift weights before classes started. Sometimes after school, T.J. lifted again.

Moe recalled that his father told him, they were not going to have any regrets. "We're going to do what we can, so when we look back, you can't say, 'I wish I would have done that,'" Dave

TIGERS

said to his son. T.J. quickly bought into The Plan. "There really wasn't a whole lot of coaxing," Dave said.

The Plan paid off with a scholarship to Missouri and a stellar career that left Moe's name in the record books. It did not, however, pay off with much of a social life. Moe managed to make it through four years in Columbia without acquiring a girlfriend. "I don't worry about that," he said his senior season. "Girls will be there. Football will not be there forever."

Words taken right out of the precepts of The Plan.

Successful living takes planning. You go to school to improve your chances for a better paying job. You use blueprints to build your home. You plan for retirement. You map out your vacation to have the best time. You even plan your children — sometimes.

Your best-laid plans, however, can get wrecked by events and circumstances beyond your control. The economy goes into the tank; a debilitating illness strikes; a hurricane hits. Life is capricious and thus no plans — not even your best ones — are foolproof.

But you don't have to go it alone. God has plans for your life that guarantee success as God defines it if you will make him your planning partner. God's plan for your life includes joy, love, peace, kindness, gentleness, and faithfulness, all the elements necessary for truly successful living for today and for all eternity. And God's plan will not fail.

[Playing football] is something you want to look back on, have no regrets [about] and be proud of for the rest of your life.
— T.J. Moe on why he stuck to The Plan

Your plans may ensure a successful life;
God's plans will ensure a successful eternity.

DAY 52

WASHED CLEAN

Read Matthew 15:1-20.

"[T]he things that come out of the mouth come from the heart, and these make a man 'unclean'" (v. 18).

So you have a laundry problem? Try washing 2,500 pounds of clothes a day as Don Barnes does during football season.

Barnes is the director of equipment operations for Mizzou's athletic department. That means he makes sure that the university's athletes in all twenty intercollegiate sports never suffer a wardrobe malfunction. As part of his duties, he runs what is in effect an industrial laundry operation. In the fall, with football in full swing, that means the equivalent of about ninety loads in a typical household washing machine each day. It works out to 225 pounds of laundry an hour.

"Baseball is by far the worst" for laundry, Barnes has said, particularly after games in states with red dirt. Equipment technician Matt Inskeep has devised a method specifically to clean the baseball pants with the most egregious stains. He attacks the offending spots with a butter knife and a power sprayer attached to a gallon jug of enzyme stain remover.

On football game weekends, Barnes and his staff spend about ten hours setting up. During a game, Barnes stations himself at the end of the bench with five trunks full of everything from duct tape to wrenches to spare jerseys. For away games, the crew packs a 48-foot tractor-trailer, preparing "for any type of weather and

TIGERS

every potential calamity." Barnes even visits a Wal-Mart before road games for a load of chewing gum for the players. "It helps calm their nerves," he said. The preferred flavor is Juicy Fruit.

Then no matter what time Barnes and his crew get home from the road, they crank up the washing machines.

"Cleanliness is next to Godliness" is one of those aphorisms that surely must come from the Bible, but you will search in vain for it there. That doesn't mean, however, that it doesn't embody a Biblical principle.

Today, as never before, we have come to understand the importance of being physically clean. We may treat it as a new idea, but it's not. Read some pertinent snippets of Numbers, and you'll find some instructions for basic hygiene, many of which the medical community took centuries to get back to.

Jesus, of course, was quite familiar with the Old Testament's proscriptions and regulations. He shocked and scandalized the religious leaders of his day, though, by asserting that spiritual cleanliness was more important than either physical or ritual cleanliness. God cares most of all about what is in our hearts, and what is inevitably there is the dark blot of sin.

Without Jesus, therefore, our worship of God, however earnest, is in vain because what God seeks before him are hearts washed clean of sin's stain. Only the saving, cleansing blood of Jesus can do that.

Laundry is my life.

— *MU equipment technician Matt Inskeep*

**Only God's saving grace in Jesus can wash
our hearts clean of the sin that stains them.**

LOSING THE WAY

Read Luke 15:11-32.

"This brother of yours was dead and is alive again; he was lost and is found" (v. 32).

Missouri's football team once got "lost" for twenty-five days.

The 1896 football season was perhaps most memorable on the field for a 115-yard touchdown run by a player named Tucker whose first name has been lost to history. It seems the goal lines at Rollins Field were 116 yards apart at the time.

The season was clearly most memorable, however, for what happened after it ended with a 3-5 record. Head coach Frank Patterson asked the university council for permission to travel to Dallas to play the athletic club. His request was denied, but since the university had no real authority over the team or its coach, he took the Tigers to Dallas anyhow. As far as the university was concerned, the team had disappeared.

The Tigers beat the Dallas club 28-0, and then two men came forward with a proposition. Missouri would play Texas in Austin and then team with the Longhorn players for a barnstorming trip that would include a foray into Mexico. Patterson readily agreed.

What followed was a jaunt that the MU yearbook said featured conduct that "was not at all times strictly decorous." The team beat Texas 10-0, the Austin Mutes 39-0, the Austin YMCA 21-10, and a San Antonio team 29-0.

The team then crossed "into Mexico over narrow-gauge railroad on private Pullmans with a special dining car." They did manage to play a couple of exhibition games in Mexico before recrossing the border. Finally, on Jan. 4, 1897, the football team ended "the best case of hooky since . . . Huckleberry Finn." They had been "lost" for 25 days and had traveled some 6,000 miles.

An unamused administration fired Patterson and suspended team captain Tom Shawhan and team manager G.H. English.

While today's navigational devices help keep us from getting lost on the highways, some of us often take wrong turns in our lives. We make bad decisions; we choose the wrong friends; we opt for what we know is a destructive lifestyle. We lose our way.

It's such a common occurrence that "being lost" is one of Christianity's most dominant metaphors. The idea is simple. The lost are those who have chosen to separate themselves from God, to live without an awareness of God in an unrepentant lifestyle contrary to his commandments and tenets. Being lost is a state of mind as much as a way of life.

It's a one-sided decision, though, since God never leaves the lost; they leave him. In God's eyes, no one is a born loser, and neither does anyone have to remain lost. Like the 1896 Missouri football team returning to Columbia, we can always turn around and find our way back to the road we should be traveling down in our lives. The way is clear: We turn back to Jesus.

The trip into Mexico . . . had to be heady stuff for the truant Tigers.
— Writer Bob Broeg on the 'lost' football team of 1896

From God's point of view, we are all either lost
or found; interestingly, we — and not God —
determine into which group we land.

DAY 54

KEEPING THE PEACE

Read Hebrews 12:14-17.

"Make every effort to live in peace with all men and to be holy" (v. 14).

Once upon a time, the Border War erupted into a brawl so severe that a reporter had blood splatter onto his jacket.

Now pretty much relegated to history by conference changes, the MU-Kansas rivalry was once so bitter and so hotly contested that it was called the Border War. The rancor crested during the 1960-61 seasons. After the Big Eight ruled Kansas had illegally recruited a football player, the league nullified KU's win over Missouri and awarded the league championship and the Orange Bowl berth to the Tigers. Kansas officials were convinced Missouri had turned them in. "On both campuses the contempt simmered."

The heat boiled over on the night of March 11 when the Tigers hosted the Jawhawks for the finale of the regular basketball season. Fearing trouble, athletic director Don Faurot stationed some football players near the floor. Several times in the first half, fans rained paper cups onto the floor in protest of calls. Just as the half ended with Missouri leading 41-37, MU's Joe Scott received a technical for leveling a Jayhawk. The crowd roared in approval.

With 14:49 left in the game, a four-month backlog of hostilities was unleashed for no immediate reason. "It was [a] whole series of events building up," said then-freshman coach Norm Stewart. After scoring a basket, Kansas' leading scorer suddenly punched

TIGERS

Mizzou's Charlie Henke right between the eyes. Benches cleared, fists flew, and fans spilled onto the floor to take part in the bedlam.

"Good gosh," exclaimed Tiger guard Terry Turlington, "there must have been 100 people on the floor." There was one less when he bopped a Kansas player on the nose. "Brother, they are really slugging in there," decreed *ABC's* announcer. The reporter for the *Missourian* had blood splatter onto his beige sports coat.

After a 10-minute delay and some ejections, the game went on without any further fisticuffs. Missouri stunned Kansas 79-76.

Perhaps you've never been in a brawl or a public brouhaha to match that of the Border War melee of March 1961. But maybe you retaliated when you got one elbow too many in a pickup basketball game. Or maybe you and your spouse or your teenager get into it occasionally, shouting and saying cruel things. Or road rage may be a part of your life.

While we do seem to live in a more belligerent, confrontational society than ever before, fighting is still not the solution to a problem. Rather, it only escalates the whole confrontation, leaving wounded pride, intransigence, and simmering hatred in its wake. Actively seeking and making peace is the way to a solution that lasts and heals broken relationships and aching hearts.

Peacemaking is not as easy as fighting, but it is certainly more courageous and a lot less painful. It is also exactly what Jesus would do.

Turned around just in time for him to smack me right between the eyes.
— Charlie Henke on the blow that began the '61 brawl

Making peace instead of fighting takes courage
and strength; it's also what Jesus would do.

HEART AND SOUL

Read Romans 12:1-2.

"Therefore, I urge you, brothers, in view of God's mercy, to offer your bodies as living sacrifices, holy and pleasing to God – this is your spiritual act of worship" (v. 1).

When Chase Daniel committed to Missouri, he stayed committed, even when the school he had always wanted to play for came calling.

Growing up in Southlake, Texas, Daniel dreamed of playing quarterback for Texas, which showed interest but never offered a scholarship. Deeply disappointed, Daniel examined the offers he was getting from all over the country. In July 2004, he picked Missouri. "It all just has a funny way of working out," Chase's mom, Vickie, said four years later. "We know in our heart of hearts, and so does Chase, that he's exactly where God put him. He's supposed to be there. There's never been a doubt. Ever."

That was abundantly clear when Texas tried to get back into the hunt a few days before national signing day in 2005. "There was no way I was going to switch," Daniel later said. "I'd already helped recruit guys who were coming [to MU]. What was I going to say to those guys? 'Oh, no, Texas came back on me late.'"

In speaking of Texas' 11th-hour inquiry, MU head coach Gary Pinkel had a simple but true explanation of why Daniel rebuffed the Horns. "It wasn't anything against Texas," he said, "but he was committed to us because we were very committed to him."

TIGERS

That reciprocal commitment worked out quite well. From 2006-08, Daniel broke virtually every Missouri passing record. His senior season, he became the school's career total offense yardage leader, passing Brad Smith. He was the Big 12 Offensive Player of the Year as a junior and the league's male athlete of the year as a senior. He quarterbacked the Tigers to thirty wins.

When you stood in a church and recited your wedding vows, did you make a decision that you could walk away from when things got tough or did you make a lifelong commitment? Is your job just a way to get a paycheck, or are you committed to it?

Commitment seems almost a dirty word in our society these days, a synonym for chains, an antonym for freedom. Perhaps this is why so many people are afraid of Jesus: Jesus demands commitment. To speak of offering yourself as "a living sacrifice" is not to speak blithely of making a decision but of heart-body-mind-and-soul commitment.

But commitment actually means "purpose and meaning," especially when you're talking about your life. Commitment makes life worthwhile; just ask Chase Daniel. Anyway, in insisting upon commitment, Jesus isn't asking anything from you that he hasn't already given to you himself. His commitment to you was so deep that he died for you.

When I committed to Missouri, I truly believed this is the place I'm going to go. I cut off all other ties.

— *Chase Daniel*

**Rather than constraining you, commitment
to Jesus lends meaning to your life,
releasing you to move forward with purpose.**

DAY 56

TOUGH COOKIES

Read 2 Corinthians 11:21b-29.

"Besides everything else, I face daily the pressure of my concern for all the churches" (v. 28).

When Larry Smith took over the Missouri football program after the 1993 season, he promised one thing for sure: the Tigers would be tougher.

Dan Devine returned to Columbia in 1992 as Mizzou's athletic director. The school had not had a winning football season since the 7-5 mark of 1983, and in hiring Smith, Devine relied on the coach's reputation for turning around struggling programs. The AD also knew he was hiring a coach much like himself, one who would rely on the running game and a tough defense.

His first day on the job, Smith promised to establish physical football at Missouri. He did. Fullback Ron Janes recalled that the first three days of Smith's initial spring practice featured nothing but running plays between the tackles. "I don't think they put in one passing play," he said. "He was just beating us up and making us tough."

One writer said practices under Smith "were Devine-like. No mercy." After a disappointing loss to Kansas in 2000, Smith had the Tigers practice in pads four straight days even though it was midseason. Fullback T.J. Leon described Missouri football under Smith as "line-it-up and smash mouth."

In 1997, Smith and his staff accomplished what was called "the

TIGERS

unthinkable" at the time: MU won seven games and landed in a bowl game. The Tigers then won eight games in 1998, including the Insight.com Bowl.

Though the success wasn't maintained, Janes said of Smith and his tough brand of football, "He restored the roar. He brought the program back to life."

You don't have to be a Missouri football player or coach to be tough. In America today, toughness isn't restricted to physical accomplishments and brute strength. Going to work every morning even when you don't feel well, sticking by your rules for your children in a society that ridicules parental authority, making hard decisions about your aging parents' care, often over their objections — you must be tough every day just to live honorably, decently, and justly.

Living faithfully requires toughness, too, though in America chances are you won't be imprisoned, stoned, or flogged this week for your faith as Paul was. Still, contemporary society exerts subtle, psychological, daily pressures on you to turn your back on your faith and your values. Popular culture promotes promiscuity, atheism, and gutter language; your children's schools have kicked God out; the corporate culture advocates amorality before the shrine of the almighty dollar.

You have to hang tough to keep the faith.

[It's] not fancy stuff. You just line up and knock the tar out of the guy over you.

— Larry Smith on playing tough, physical football

Life demands more than mere physical toughness; you must be spiritually tough too.

WHOLEHEARTEDLY

Read 1 Samuel 13:1-14.

"The Lord has sought out a man after his own heart" (v. 14).

The Tigers were in real trouble. What let them escape wasn't just talent; it was also a whole lot of heart.

On Oct. 12, 2013, the 5-0 and 25th-ranked Tigers took on 7th-ranked Georgia in Athens. Early on, Missouri had its way, leading by 18 points at halftime. Then came one setback after another that left the Tigers in a really bad predicament.

Georgia rallied, scoring sixteen straight points to cut the once-comfortable lead to 28-26 early in the fourth quarter. Missouri's "defense was getting gashed and Sanford Stadium was roaring so loud that Coach Gary Pinkel couldn't hear the voices in his headset." It got worse.

Missouri's do-it-all senior quarterback, James Franklin, who was so tough he had earned the nickname "Frank the Tank," suddenly ran out of bounds instead of barreling for more yardage. That was a sign something was wrong. It turned out to be very wrong: Franklin had a separated shoulder.

That left this pivotal game — one that would truly "validate the Tigers as full card-carrying members of the SEC" — in the hands of redshirt freshman Maty Mauk. His season had so far consisted of handing off during mop-up time of blowouts.

Missouri called a timeout, and quarterbacks coach Andy Hill

huddled with Mauk to talk over plays. On his first snap, Mauk pulled off a perfect quarterback draw and got a first down. Two plays later, wide receiver Bud Sasser rifled a bullet to L'Damian Washington for a 40-yard touchdown.

That took the heart out of the Bulldogs. Randy Ponder grabbed an interception, setting up a Henry Josey score. MU won 41-26.

"When we see adversity, our defense mechanism is to tighten up to each other," declared left guard Max Copeland. In other words, when the going got tough, the Tigers showed their heart.

We all stare into the cold, hard face of defeat as the Tigers did that Saturday against Georgia. Unlike MU that day, though, we sometimes fight with all we have and all our heart and still lose.

You probably can recall a time when you admitted you were whipped no matter how much it hurt. Always in your life, though, you have known that you would fight for some things with all your heart and never give them up no matter the cost: your family, your country, your friends, your core beliefs.

God should be on that list too. God seeks men and women who will never turn their back on him because they are people after God's own heart. That is, they will never betray God with their unbelief; they will never lose their childlike trust in God; they will never cease to love God with all their heart.

They are lifetime members of God's team; it's a mighty good one to be on, but it takes heart.

These guys battle, man. They've got a lot of heart.
— Gary Pinkel after the 2013 win over Georgia

**To be on God's team requires
the heart of a champion.**

THE SUB

Read Galatians 3:10-14.

"Christ redeemed us from the curse of the law by becoming a curse for us" (v. 13).

It was over and done. Missouri's bid for "a miraculous win at Ann Arbor" had come up short. And then a sub stepped up.

The Tigers were big underdogs on Sept. 26, 1959, against the Michigan Wolverines. But a 46-yard run by halfback Mel West and a 36-yard strike from quarterback Phil Snowden to Dale Pidcock — plus some staunch defense — propelled the Tigers to a 14-12 lead in the fourth quarter. The Wolverines apparently saved themselves, though, when they took their first lead of the game on a field goal with 2:49 left to play.

The Tigers had a bigger problem than the clock. Under the limited substitution rule in play, Snowden could not come back into the game. That meant Bob Haas — "a defensive star with limited ability as a passer" — was under center. He had starred on defense that day with a pair of interceptions, but Haas himself admitted that he wasn't a potent passer.

Here he was, though, taking over the huddle at the Missouri 22 in what amounted to a race against the clock.

Haas promptly completed a pass to end Danny LaRose for 12 yards. West picked up 11, and Haas hit Rose again. On fourth and 5, Haas was flushed out of the pocket as he tried to pass and scrambled for 13 yards to the Michigan 38.

TIGERS

With only 1:10 on the clock, the incredible sub did it again. He delivered a strike to end Donnie Smith between two Michigan defenders down to the 3-yard line. With the clock running and no time outs, West made it to the 1 on a pair of dives before Haas sneaked in with two seconds on the clock. Missouri won 20-15.

Despite his inexperience, Haas the super sub had completed three clutch passes in leading his team on an 11-play, 78-yard scoring drive in less than three minutes.

Wouldn't it be cool if you had a substitute like Bob Haas for all life's hard stuff? Telling of a death in the family? Call in your sub. Breaking up with your boyfriend? Job interview? Chemistry test? Crucial presentation at work? Let the sub handle it.

We do have such a substitute, but not for the matters of life. Instead, Jesus is our substitute for matters of life and death. Since Jesus has already made it, we don't have to make the sacrifice God demands for forgiveness and salvation.

One of the most pathetic aspects of our contemporary times is that many people deny Jesus Christ and then desperately cast about for a substitute for him. Mysticism, human philosophies such as Scientology, false religions such as Hinduism and Islam, cults, New Age approaches that preach self-fulfillment without responsibility or accountability — they and others like them are all pitiful, inadequate substitutes for Jesus.

There is no substitute for Jesus. It's Jesus or nothing.

That was the greatest clutch performance I've ever seen.
— Dan Devine to Bob Haas after the '59 Michigan game

**There is no substitute for Jesus,
the consummate substitute.**

PRACTICE SESSION

Read 2 Peter 1:3-11.

"For if you do these things, you will never fail, and you will receive a rich welcome into the eternal kingdom of our Lord and Savior Jesus Christ" (vv. 10b-11).

In what may well be the unlikeliest season in MU men's basketball history, what appeared to be the season's unlikeliest shot wasn't. That's because the Tigers practiced it.

Nobody — not even the players — saw what happened in 2008-09 coming. "I wouldn't have laughed, necessarily, but I would have been like, 'Seriously?'" said senior guard Matt Lawrence when asked if he could have forecasted back in November what the season would bring.

Picked to finish seventh in the Big 12, the team set a school record with 31 wins and finished third in the league and ranked in the top ten. They then won the league tournament for the first time ever and drew a third seed in the NCAA Tournament.

The Tigers beat Cornell and Marquette to advance to the Sweet 16 against the second-seeded Tigers from Memphis. There they simply blew past Memphis 102-91 to advance to the Elite Eight for the fourth time in school history.

One play — one shot — illustrated the magic of the season and the talent of the team. Memphis scored with five seconds left in the first half. Freshman MU guard Marcus Denmon took the inbounds pass from Justin Safford and let fly from well beyond the midcourt line. The shot hit nothing but net, sending MU into the locker room with a 49-36 lead and all the momentum.

Luck? Not at all. At the end of every practice, the Tigers simulated a last-second desperation shot. Denmon showed a knack for making them. "He's definitely the best half-court-and-beyond shooter on our team," Lawrence said.

The Tigers practiced for just such a chance.

Imagine a football team that never practices. A play cast that doesn't rehearse. A preacher who never studies the Bible before he delivers a message. When the showdown comes, they would be revealed as inept bumblers that merit our disdain.

We practice something so that we will become good at it, so that it becomes so natural that we can pull it off without even having to think about it. Interestingly, if we are to live as Christ wants us to, then we must practice that lifestyle, and showing up at church and sitting stoically on a pew once a week does not constitute practice. To practice successfully, we must participate; we must do repeatedly whatever it is we want to be good at.

We must practice being like Christ by living like Christ every day of our lives. For Christians, practice is a lifestyle that doesn't make perfect — only Christ is perfect — but it does prepare us for the real thing: the day we meet God face to face and inherit Christ's kingdom.

It was a great shot, and he makes it at least once a week in practice.
— Guard Kim English on Marcus Denmon's shot vs. Memphis

Practicing the Christian lifestyle doesn't
make us perfect, but it does secure us
a permanent place beside the perfect one.

DAY 60

THE FAME GAME

Read 1 Kings 10:1-10, 18-29.

*"King Solomon was greater in riches and wisdom than
all the other kings of the earth. The whole world sought
audience with Solomon" (vv. 23-24).*

How in the world could Van Robinson ever hope to be famous
when the media couldn't get his name right for decades?

Robinson was only 16 years old and weighed all of 165 pounds
when he began his football career at Missouri. "I would not be
big enough to be a water boy now," he admitted. But this was
1943 and World War II was raging. Missouri "had trouble getting
players," Robinson said.

Nevertheless, the undersized end lettered in 1944. In the 28-0
win over Kansas, he had a rather unusual interception. The game
was played at the home of a minor-league baseball team, and the
pitcher's mound hadn't been leveled. Robinson recalled running
up the mound where he was tackled. He told his coach, "I felt like
I was running uphill." Coach Herb Bunker replied, "Robinson, I
feel like you have been running uphill all season."

The highlight of his career came in the 21-21 tie with Oklahoma
that season. With Missouri trailing 21-7 in the third quarter, he
ignited a rally with an interception and a 60-yard return.

To Robinson's dismay, the headline in a Kansas City newspaper
reported that "Stan Robinson," rather than "Van Robinson," had
an interception that set up a Tiger touchdown. The fame-busting

120   DAY 60

error wouldn't go away. In 1969, Robinson bought a program at a Missouri game and found a recount of that '44 game. He was still called "Stan Robinson." "Twenty-five years later, and it's a journalism school, and they still didn't get it right," Robinson said. It only got worse. A correction was subsequently run that called him "Van Morrison," as in the Irish pop/folk singer.

Have you ever wanted to be famous? Hanging out with other rich and famous people, having folks with microphones listen to what you say, throwing money around like toilet paper, meeting adoring and clamoring fans, signing autographs, and posing for the paparazzi before you climb into your imported sports car?

Many of us yearn to be famous, well-known in the places and by the people that we believe matter. That's all fame amounts to: strangers knowing your name and your face.

The truth is that you are already famous where it really does matter, which excludes TV's talking heads, screaming teenagers, rapt moviegoers, or D.C. power brokers. You are famous because Almighty God knows your name, your face, and everything else there is to know about you.

If a persistent photographer snapped you pondering this fame — the only kind that has eternal significance — would the picture show the world unbridled joy or the shell-shocked expression of a mug shot?

It was my greatest accomplishment and they misspelled my name.
— Van Robinson on his interception vs. Oklahoma

**You're already famous because God knows
your name and your face, which may
be either reassuring or terrifying.**

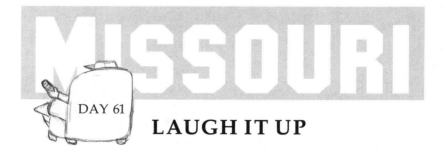

DAY 61

LAUGH IT UP

Read Genesis 21:1-7.

"Sarah said, 'God has brought me laughter, and everyone who hears about this will laugh with me'" (v. 6).

Missouri head coach Dan Devine was a master motivator who often used psychological ploys to get his team fired up. Sometimes, though, his efforts missed their mark, drawing only laughter or funny responses from his players.

With the Nebraska game up next, tackle Francis Peay, who would be a first-round draft pick, one day opened his locker and found a cornhusk in it. He had no idea what it was. Trainer Fred Wappel had to clue him in and tell him why it was in the locker. "It's just a reminder about the big game from the coach," he said. "Good thing we ain't playing the Chicago Bears," Peay replied.

Safety Dennis Poppe, who was All-Big Eight as a senior in 1969 and later served as assistant athletic director at MU, recalled that the week of the Oklahoma game in '69 the players discovered a record player in the training room. Devine played "Boomer Sooner" on it over and over each day. "On Thursday during our walk through," Poppe said, "all of a sudden we hear the scraping sound of a needle on a record." The room then got real quiet.

Standing in the middle of the locker room, Devine said, "I hope you are tired of the record!" Then he tried to break it over a knee, but the vinyl refused to snap. Finally, the frustrated head coach gave up and slung the record about twenty feet.

TIGERS

"We all are laughing so hard and trying to get out of the locker room because we didn't want him to see us laughing," Poppe said. "He was a master motivational type of guy. We knew what he was trying to do."

This particular ploy may not have turned out quite as the head Tiger wanted it to since it left the players laughing, but something about it worked. Two days later, Missouri went out and buried Oklahoma and its Heisman-Trophy winner Steve Owens 44-10.

Stand-up comedians are successful because they find humor in the world, and it's often hard for us to do that. "Laughter is foolish," an acerbic Solomon wrote in Ecclesiastes 2:2, his angst overwhelming him because he couldn't find much if anything in his world to laugh at.

We know how he felt. When we take a good look around at this world we live in, can we really find much to laugh at? It seems everywhere we look we find not just godlessness but ongoing and pervasive tragedy and misery.

Well, we can recognize as Sarah did that in God's innumerable gifts lie irresistible laughter. The great gift of Jesus provides us with more than enough reason to laugh no matter our situation. Through God's grace in Jesus Christ, we can laugh at death, at Satan, at the very gates of hell, at the world's pain.

Because they are of this world, our tears will pass. Because it is of God, our laughter will remain — forever.

Cultivate cheerfulness.

— *Knute Rockne*

**Of the world, sorrow is temporary;
of God, laughter is forever.**

OUT OF CHARACTER

Read Mark 6:1-6.

"'Isn't this Mary's son, and the brother of James, Joseph, Judas and Simon. Aren't his sisters here with us?' And they took offense at him" (v. 3).

The Tigers garnered their first SEC win by playing completely out of character.

Since he began his head coaching career at Toledo in 1991, Gary Pinkel had pretty much "hit the jackpot at football's most important position." As writer Dave Matter put, it, "Some seasons, he might have 99 problems — but a quarterback ain't one." And then 2012 came along.

Starting quarterback James Franklin needed shoulder surgery in the offseason and then was injured twice during the season. For the first time since 2001, his first season in Columbia, Pinkel had to start his backup.

That backup made his third start on Oct. 27 when the Kentucky Wildcats came to town. A bunch of injuries teamed with the rugged SEC competition to leave the Tigers still looking for their first win in their new conference.

MU led 17-10 in the third quarter, but after a pair of interceptions, Pinkel made an out-of-character decision. For the first time in his career at Missouri, he benched his starting quarterback in a game that was competitive. He put Franklin in though he was still nursing a sprained knee ligament and wearing a brace.

TIGERS

Franklin's injury limited him to a caretaker role, forcing the Tigers into a game plan that was completely out of character. Pinkel and his coaches eliminated quarterback runs, play-action passes, and long-developing throws. They went to power football, a run-at-all-costs approach — and it worked.

On a day when Missouri threw for just 87 yards — the fewest for the program since a win over Baylor in 2005 — the top three backs ran for 188 yards and three touchdowns on 38 carries. Kendial Lawrence led the attack with 108 yards and two scores on 23 carries. The Tigers ran to their first SEC win in a 33-10 romp.

Over time, people who know you well expect you to behave a certain way. Thus, you totally flummox your friends and family members when you haul off and do something out of character as the Tigers did against UK by becoming a running team. In your case, maybe you bought a flashy new car, got your hair cut short or changed the color altogether, or suddenly changed jobs.

Maybe you even reinvigorated or discovered your faith life.

Acting out of character when it comes to your faith is exactly what you want to do. It is, in fact, the most revealing mark of a person who is serious about his or her walk with Jesus, whether it's a new hiker or an experienced trekker making the trip.

That's because the goal for a Christian really is a change in character. You seek not to act like yourself anymore. Rather, you emulate the ideal. You act like Jesus instead.

You do what's the best call for your team.
— Gary Pinkel on his out-of-character game plan vs. Kentucky

To be serious about Jesus is to act out of character; rather than acting like yourself, you act like him.

MYSTERIOUS WAYS

Read Romans 11:25-36.

"O the depth of the riches and wisdom and knowledge of God! How unsearchable are his judgments and how inscrutable his ways!" (v. 33 NRSV)

Lana Mims knows full well that the mysterious ways of God led her to Missouri.

Mims' path to MU was downright byzantine. The daughter of four-time Olympian Madeline Mims and the sister of an OU triple-jump champion, Mims not surprisingly was a track star in high school, a three-time state champion. She verbally committed to one Big-12 school, but looked elsewhere when circumstances changed in the athletic department. An SEC school recruited her and backed off at the last minute. Another ran out of money and dropped its offer. "So many doors just slammed shut," Mims said.

By what was described as "some small miracle," Mizzou track coach Rick McGuire had kept a scholarship for her even though she had turned the Tigers down. Thus, almost as a last resort, she headed to Columbia, a place she'd never expected to live.

Mims soon realized that she was at Missouri because God had put her there. She arrived in the fall of 2006 full of promise and ambition but developed heart problems in 2007 that required a corrective procedure. It was unsuccessful, leaving her feeling ill and suffering from migraines.

Mims mended, but before her senior year of 2009-10, her heart acted up again, necessitating more surgery. Despite her travails, Mims saw God's hand on her. "If it were any other school," she said, "my scholarship probably would have been taken away. I know I've been blessed to be at the University of Missouri."

Her scholarship intact, in 2010 she finished her Tiger career as a member of the school's record-setting 4x400m relay team and as a five-time All-Big 12 honoree in jumps and sprints.

People of faith such as Lana Mims understand that the good Lord does indeed work in mysterious ways. This only serves to make God even more tantalizing because human nature loves a good mystery. We relish the challenge of uncovering what somebody else wants to hide. We are intrigued by *NCIS*, a rousing round of Clue, or *Matlock* reruns.

Some mysteries are simply beyond our knowing or solving, however. Events in our lives that are in actuality the mysterious ways of God remain so to us because we can't see the divine machinations. We can see only the results, appreciate that God was behind it all, and give him thanks and praise.

God has revealed much about himself, especially through Jesus, but still much remains unknowable. Why does he tolerate the existence of evil? What does he really look like? Why is he so fond of bugs? What was the inspiration for chocolate?

We know for sure, though, that God is love, and so we proceed with life, assured that one day all mysteries will be revealed.

I can look back and see that God had a reason for bringing me here.
— Lana Mims on winding up at Missouri

God keeps much about himself shrouded in mystery, but one day we will see and understand.

KEEP OUT!

Read Exodus 26:31-35; 30:1-10.

"The curtain will separate the Holy Place from the Most Holy Place" (v. 26:33).

The Tigers just weren't interested in the kicker who would eventually have the greatest season in the history of college football.

Grant Ressel attempted only six field goals his senior season of high school and received absolutely no interest from recruiters. He spent most of the year letting the MU coaches know he was interested in walking on. He finally received a visit from David Yost, MU's offensive coordinator and kicking coach, who, Ressel recalled, "said something about walking on." So he figured the Tigers were going to let him walk on.

But Ressel didn't hear a word from anybody associated with the football program even after he arrived on campus in the fall of 2007. "I get here the first week of school and still haven't heard from [the coaches]," he recalled. "I was like, 'Well, I guess I'm still trying out for the team.'" Finally, he got a call that let him know tryouts were that afternoon. "I'm like, 'OK, that's good notice."

Ressel competed against seven other kickers at the tryout and thought he performed quite well. All he got for his trouble was a message that the team didn't need him. "We don't have any spots available in the locker room," it said.

So the unwanted would-be kicker watched the season from the stands and sent out e-mails to most other major college programs.

That got the coaches' attention. "He started talking about transferring somewhere else to kick," Yost said. "That's when we said, 'OK, we don't want him to go do that.'"

Ressel was finally allowed to walk on. He apprenticed under All-Big 12 kicker Jeff Wolfert and then won the starting job before the 2009 season. All this barely noticed and virtually unwanted kicker did in 2009 was set the all-time NCAA record for combined kicking accuracy by nailing 26-of-27 field goals and 39-of-39 PATs. He was first-team All-America.

That civic club that secures its membership by invitation only. The bleachers where you sit while others frolic in the sky boxes. That neighborhood you can't afford a house in. Like Grant Ressel, you know all about being shut out of some club, some group, or some place. "Exclusive" is the word that keeps you out.

The Hebrew people, too, knew about being told to keep out; only the high priest enter the Most Holy Place — which housed the ark — and survive. Then along came Jesus to kick that barrier down and give us direct access to God.

In the process, though, Jesus created another exclusive club; its members are his followers, Christians, those who believe he is the Son of God and the savior of the world. This club, though, extends a membership invitation to everyone in the whole wide world; no one is excluded. Whether you're in or out depends on your response to Jesus, not on arbitrary gatekeepers.

Don't know what's going on. They don't answer your calls or anything.
— Grant Ressel on not hearing anything from the MU coaches in 2007

**Christianity is an exclusive club, but an invitation
is extended to everyone and no one is denied entry.**

PROBLEM CHILD

Read James 1:2-12.

"Blessed is the man who perseveres under trial, because when he has stood the test, he will receive the crown of life that God has promised to those who love him" (v. 12).

Leave it to a head football coach to find a problem after his team has slaughtered Nebraska 52-17 on the road.

On Oct. 3, 2008, the fourth-ranked Tigers "purg[ed] a 15-game, 30-year streak of indignities and torments in one of the nation's football cathedrals." The win was MU's second straight romp over Nebraska. In 2007, they mauled the Huskers 41-6 in Columbia. After that game, MU quarterback Chase Daniel called Nebraska's unwillingness to change defenses "high school stuff." This time around the Cornhuskers "insisted all week they had numerous schemes to foil Mizzou."

They didn't. Only three plays and 59 seconds into the game, Daniel hit sophomore wide receiver Jeremy Maclin for a 58-yard touchdown. Maclin would be a two-time All-America; in 2006, he had set the NCAA record for all-purpose yards by a freshman.

After Nebraska scored to tie the game, Missouri responded with an 80-yard drive. When Jeff Wolfert booted a 48-yard field goal, Missouri led 17-7 and the Huskers were done.

Senior linebacker Brock Christopher intercepted a pass and returned it 17 yards for a touchdown that propelled Missouri into a 31-7 lead at halftime. Two more Daniel touchdown tosses and another score put the Tigers up 52-10 before the third quarter was over. The Huskers were just no problem at all.

"They wanted to shut us down," Daniel remarked. "I think that ended within a minute of the game (starting)."

And that problem Gary Pinkel detected in the 52-17 win? Only a head coach would regard it as a situation that would require some work at practice. The Tigers never had to punt.

Problems are such a ubiquitous feature of our lives that a whole day — twenty-four hours — without a single problem ranks right up there with a government without taxes; a Missouri team that never, ever loses a game; and entertaining, wholesome television programs. We just can't even imagine it.

But that's life. Even Jesus had his share of problems, especially with his twelve-man staff. Jesus could have easily removed all problems from his daily walk, but what good would that have done us? Our goal is to become like Jesus, and we could never fashion ourselves after a man who didn't encounter job stress, criticism, loneliness, temptation, frustration, and discouragement.

Instead, Jesus showed us that when — not if — problems come, a person of faith uses them to get better rather than letting the problems use him to get bitter. We learn God-filled perseverance and patience as we develop and deepen our faith and our trust in God. Problems will pass; eternity will not.

We're going to have to work on it in practice, because that's not reality.
— Gary Pinkel on not punting against Nebraska

The problem with problems is that we often
let them use us and become bitter
rather than using them to become better.

DOWN AND DIRTY

Read Isaiah 1:15-20.

"Though your sins are like scarlet, they shall be as white as snow; though they are red as crimson, they shall be like wool" (v. 18).

School officials hoped to have a pristine stadium to show off when Memorial Stadium opened. Instead, they wound up with a mudhole.

In 1891 a field was set aside for athletics, but it wasn't useful for several years. The Rollins brothers of Columbia donated funds for a cinder track and did the grading and leveling of the field, and the school's engineering students built wooden bleachers. A wall and concrete bleachers were later constructed. The field was formally dedicated as "Rollins Field" at the Kansas game of 1911.

The facility held only 13,000 people, and a new stadium was soon needed as interest in football grew. Thus, Memorial Stadium was constructed in a natural valley that lay to the south of the university.

According to Art Nebel, a student at the time who later served as a school dean, a blast during the construction buried a rock crusher and a truck. "They're still down there under the gridiron," Nebel said in the 1970s.

Plans called for the new facility to be used for the first time on Oct. 2, 1926, against Tulane. Three days before the game, however, an ongoing deluge washed out a bridge, requiring some feverish

TIGERS

repair work by the state highway department.

The bridge was readied in time for the big day; the field was not. The steady downpour meant the playing surface had not been sodded. What the players stepped onto was sawdust and bark that had been spread around. A two-hour rainstorm finished the job of turning the field into one big mudhole.

Rendered hapless, the players managed only a scoreless tie.

Maybe you've never slopped any pigs and thus have never traipsed around a "hog wallow." You may not be a fan of mud boggin'. Still, you've worked on your car, planted a garden, played touch football in the rain, or endured some military training. You've been dirty.

Dirt, grime, and mud aren't the only sources of stains, however. We can also get dirty spiritually by not living in accordance with God's commands, by doing what's wrong, or by not doing what's right. We all experience temporary shortcomings and failures; we all slip and fall into the mud.

Whether we stay there or not, though, is a function of our relationship with Jesus. For the followers of Jesus, sin is not a way of life; it's an abnormality, so we don't stay in the filth. We seek a spiritual bath by expressing regret and asking for God's pardon in Jesus' name. God responds by washing our soul white as snow with his forgiveness.

The game was scoreless — a mudpie tie.
— Writer Bob Broeg on the first game played at Memorial Stadium

**When your soul gets dirty, a powerful and
thorough cleansing agent is available
for the asking: God's forgiveness.**

DAY 67

COMEBACK KIDS

Read Luke 23:26-43.

"Jesus answered him, 'I tell you the truth, today you will be with me in paradise'" (v. 43).

The comeback the Missouri women pulled off against Texas in 2011 was so incredible it bordered on the ridiculous.

The meeting of Jan. 8 at Mizzou Arena went pretty much as everyone expected. Texas was ranked 22nd, and the Tigers were still finding their way under first-year coach Robin Pingeton and were coming off a pair of 32-point losses. With 2:26 to play, Texas led 72-60.

"I thought the game was pretty much over," said Texas head coach Gail Goestenkors. She and everyone else. Missouri had used only seven players to that point, and the Tigers "were visibly gassed." "We thought we had the game sewn up," declared one Longhorn. But what happened after that was a "wild flurry of circumstances Goestenkors said she had never experienced in her 26-year coaching career."

Nobody got too excited when senior forward RaeShara Brown hit a pair of free throws and junior forward Christine Flores hit a layup. After all, the Tigers still trained 72-64 with 1:06 to play.

But Flores hit a three-pointer and Texas missed a pair of free throws. The faithful who still remained suddenly got very interested in what was going on. When Flores nailed another trey, the place went nuts.

TIGERS

Texas blew a layup, and the Tigers came downcourt looking for the tie. They got it, going inside to senior forward Shakara Jones, who powered it home with 22 seconds left.

When Texas missed a pair of jumpers in the final seconds, regulation ended with a stunning 72-72 tie. In overtime, senior guard Jasmyn Otote, who finished with 14 points, hit a three, her fourth of the game, to break a 74-74 tie. Missouri never trailed again and finished off one of the most incredible comebacks in program history with an 85-80 win.

"They kept playing and we didn't," said one Texas player.

Life will have its setbacks whether they result from personal failures or from forces and people beyond your control. Being a Christian and a faithful follower of Jesus Christ doesn't insulate you from getting into deep trouble. Maybe financial problems suffocated you. Or your family was hit with a great tragedy. Life is a series of victories and defeats. Winning isn't about avoiding defeat; it's about getting back up to compete again. It's about making a comeback of your own.

When you avail yourself of God's grace and God's power, your comeback is always greater than your setback. You are never too far behind, and it's never too late in life's game for Jesus to lead you to victory, to turn trouble into triumph. As it was with the Missouri women against Texas and the thief on the cross who repented, it's not how you start that counts; it's how you finish.

I didn't see any quit in our kids.
— Robin Pingeton on being behind vs. Texas

**No matter the circumstances in your life,
you can begin a comeback by turning to Jesus.**

BAD IDEA

Read Mark 14:43-50.

"The betrayer had arranged a signal with them: 'The one I kiss is the man; arrest him and lead him away under guard'" (v. 44).

Beau Brinkley had an idea that Gary Pinkel at first rejected outright as simply horrible. After the head Tiger thought about it for a while, though, he decided it wasn't such a bad idea after all.

Brinkley earned a scholarship at Missouri based solely on his ability to snap a football a long distance. He walked on in 2008 and was named the team's Walk-On MVP. As a sophomore in 2009, Brinkley had a season that few players in football history could claim; it was described as "virtually flawless." His on-target snaps helped first-year kicker Grant Ressel set an NCAA single-season kicking accuracy record for combined kicks. Brinkley was MU's Special Teams Player of the Year.

From the first, though, Brinkley had an idea that he couldn't shake: He wanted to do more than just snap for kicks. He went to former Tiger wide receiver Tommy Saunders for advice, and Saunders came up with a pretty good idea. He told Brinkley to first establish himself as the long snapper. Meanwhile, he would lead Brinkley through the receivers' route-running sessions each day after practice. Brinkley doggedly pursued his idea; every day in 2008, he worked out some on his own as a receiver.

In the spring of 2009, Brinkley approached Pinkel with his idea, which he presented as a request. "He wanted to snap *and* play at a position," Pinkel said. Fearing injury to a valuable special teams member, the head coach was firm with his answer. "Beau, you're not going to do that," he said.

He reconsidered, though, and told Brinkley they would let him work some at receiver and tight end while he still held down all the long snapping chores. The idea that was so bad at first blush turned out to be a pretty good one. Before the fourth game of the '09 season, Brinkley was named the team's starting tight end.

That sure-fire investment you made from a pal's hot stock tip. The expensive exercise machine that now traps dust bunnies under your bed. Blond hair. Telling your wife you wanted to eat at the restaurant with the waitresses in the skimpy shorts. They seemed like pretty good ideas at the time; they weren't.

We all have bad ideas in our lifetime. They provide some of our most crucial learning experiences. Gary Pinkel found himself a tight end from what he at first thought was a bad idea.

Some ideas, though, are so irreparably and inherently bad that we cannot help but wonder why they were even conceived in the first place. Almost two thousand years ago a man had just such an idea. Judas' betrayal of Jesus remains to this day one of the most heinous acts of treachery in history.

Turning his back on Jesus was a bad idea for Judas then; it's a bad idea for us now.

Who would have thought I'd be out here where I am right now?
— Beau Brinkley on seeing his bad idea work out

We all have some bad ideas in our lives; nothing equals the folly of turning away from Jesus.

NAME DROPPING

Read Exodus 3:13-20.

"God said to Moses, 'I AM WHO I AM. This is what you are to say to the Israelites: 'I AM has sent me to yo'''' (v. 14).

Head coach Dan Devine willingly supplied his own nickname to beat writers: "fussbudget." His preoccupied ritual one afternoon at practice showed just how apt the moniker was.

An Irish choir boy who grew up in Minnesota, Devine coached the Tigers from 1958-70 and won 93 games. His .704 winning percentage remains the best in MU history of any coach with more than two seasons in Columbia.

With a mother who was not strong and a father who was ill, Devine was raised by an aunt who backed up his self-professed nickname. "He was so particular," she once said. "It's no wonder he has such lovely hair and teeth. He brushed them constantly."

Writer Bob Broeg wrote that when the boy became a man, "Dapper Dan became an antiseptic germ-chaser, a natural target for gags." Perhaps at no single time were Devine's "fussbudgety" tendencies so illustrated as one afternoon at practice when, Broeg wrote, "he outdid himself in his ritual."

It helped that Devine at the time was preoccupied with his practice plans. Thus, he probably didn't really notice what he was doing as he prepared for his team's workout. "He pulled a whistle out of his windbreaker, dropped it in alcohol, washed his hands,

TIGERS

gargled, combed his hair, washed and rinsed the whistle, dried it, dropped it back in his pocket, and trotted out to the field."

Not surprisingly, all those gyrations caught the attention of the assistant coaches. Next morning, his staff presented him with a gallon of mouthwash.

Nicknames such as Dan Devine's 'Fussbudget' are not slapped haphazardly upon individuals but rather reflect widely held perceptions about the person named. Proper names can also have a particular physical or character trait associated with them.

Nowhere throughout the long march of history has this concept been more prevalent than in the Bible, where a name is not a mere label but is an expression of the essential nature of the one who is named. That is, a person's name reveals much about his or her character. This applies even to God; to know the name of God is to know God as he has chosen to reveal himself to us.

What does your name say about you? Honest, trustworthy, a seeker of the truth and a person of God? Or does the mention of your name cause your coworkers to whisper snide remarks, your neighbors to roll their eyes, or your friends to start making allowances for you?

Most importantly, what does your name say about you to God? He, too, knows you by name.

If you're looking for a word for me, I'll save you the trouble. I'm what you would call a 'fussbudget.'

— *Dan Devine*

**Live so that your name evokes positive
associations by people you know,
by the public, and by God.**

THE BIG TIME

Read Revelation 21:22-27; 22:1-6.

"They will see his face, and his name will be on their foreheads. . . . And they will reign for ever and ever" (vv. 22:4, 5c).

The Missouri Tigers hit the big time on Nov. 11, 1939.

The university's athletes had pretty much labored amid the obscurity that blanketed any program not favored by the Eastern media. The first inklings of publicity and reputation for Mizzou came during the 1938 season with the play of sophomore quarterback Paul Christman, a two-time All-America who would finish third in the voting for the Heisman Trophy in 1939.

The Tigers were 5-1 when they stepped off the train and into the spotlight that November weekend in New York City. They were on the country's biggest stage to take on the 17th-ranked Violets of New York University in Yankee Stadium.

Many of the nation's premier sportswriters were on hand. As much as anything, curiosity about this quarterback from halfway across the country drove them there. Christman did not disappoint. He "emerged as one of college football's brightest stars," and the Tigers stepped right up into the big time.

As one writer put it, Christman played "with all the nonchalance of a coed powdering her nose at the junior prom." Oblivious to all the pressure and the big stage, Christman personally outgained the entire NYU team in a 20-7 Mizzou win. "The big kid

TIGERS

from corn country stole the show," wrote *The New York Times*. But it wasn't just Christman that bedazzled New York; it was the whole Missouri team.

Appreciating the significance of the win, more than 2,000 MU students braved 16-degree weather to welcome the victors when their train rolled into Columbia. The win propelled Missouri to a No.-12 AP ranking, its first-ever Top-20 appearance.

The Tigers had hit the big time.

Like college sports programs, we often look around at our current situation and dream of hitting the big time. We might look longingly at that vice-president's office or daydream about the day when we're the boss, maybe even of our own business. We may scheme about ways to make a lot of money, or at least more than we're making now. We may even consciously seek out fame and power.

Making it big is just part of the American dream. It's the heart of that which drives immigrants to leave everything they know and come to this country.

The truth, though, is that all of this so-called "big-time" stuff we so earnestly cherish is actually only small potatoes. If we want to speak of what is the real big-time, we better think about God and his dwelling place in Heaven. There we not only see God and Jesus face to face, but we reign. God puts us in charge.

One game, more than any other, established Mizzou's national prominence.
— Todd Donoho and Dan O'Brien on the win over NYU

Living with God, hanging out with Jesus,
and reigning in Heaven — now that's big time.

ON THE MONEY

Read Luke 16:1-15.

"You cannot serve both God and money" (v. 13b).

Money problems were on a totally different scale in the earliest days of the Missouri football program, back when the team showed a $100 profit from a game and bought new uniforms with the money.

Still known as Missouri State University in 1890, the school found itself flush with money after the program's first-ever game, against Washington University in St. Louis. (See Devotion No. 1). The $100 the team netted from the game was enough to outfit the squad with new uniforms. That same year the first general athletic association was formed; it was controlled by the students, 62 of whom willingly paid a $1 initiation fee.

With interest in the school's athletics soaring, the university's women's club put on a preseason show and raised $232.50 for the football team prior to the 1893 season. H.O. Robinson, a student serving as coach, used the money to set up a training table in a small cottage he rented. Seventeen players ate there, consuming 26 pounds of meat a day. The cost was $3 per week per player.

By 1895, admission prices to Missouri's games ranged from 25 cents for the opener against the Sedalia Athletic Club to $1 and up for the Kansas game at Kansas City. With athletic funds sagging in 1896, ticket prices were boosted to $2.50 each for the four home games. As a bonus to encourage purchases, the tickets granted

TIGERS

the holder access to the team's practice sessions.

The 5-3 season of 1902 solved a lot of financial problems. The Tigers cleared $3,500 alone from the Kansas game. Expenses in 1903 totaled about $5,000; the training table for the whole season was only $400 while gate guarantees and officials' expenses were another $1,800.

Football money was tight in those early days, but by 1904 John F. McLean was paid the whopping sum of $2,000 to coach.

Having a little too much money at the end of the month may be as bothersome — if not as worrisome — as having a little too much month at the end of the money. The investment possibilities are both bewildering and seemingly endless.

You take your money seriously, as well you should. Jesus, too, took money seriously, warning us frequently of its dangers. In fact, Jesus spoke more often about money than he did of Heaven and Hell combined.

Money itself isn't evil; it's neutral. Its peril lies in the ease with which it can usurp God's rightful place as the master of our lives.

Certainly in our age and society, we often measure people by how much money they have. But like our other talents, gifts, and resources, money should primarily be used for God's purposes. God's love must touch not only our hearts but our wallets also.

How much of your wealth are you investing with God?

As usual, in 1896, there was a new coach . . . because Missouri did not like paying $500 to $700 a month [to] Pop Bliss — for two months..
— Bob Broeg on tight money for football in the early days

Your attitude about money says much
about your attitude toward God.

DREAM WORLD

Read Joshua 3.

"All Israel passed by until the whole nation had completed the crossing on dry ground" (v. 17b).

Kim Anderson was riding a bicycle when he learned he was in the running for the dream job he had given up on.

Anderson spent fifteen years at Missouri as a player and an assistant coach under Norm Stewart. He was the 1977 Big Eight Player of the Year and was a star on the '76 team, which won the first of Stewart's eight conference titles. He was an assistant coach in 1994 when Missouri went 14-0 in the Big Eight, won the last of Stewart's league titles, and made a run to the Elite Eight.

Anderson was Stewart's top assistant coach when the MU legend retired in 1999. He interviewed for the job but was passed over in favor of Quin Snyder. He took the head job at Central Missouri in 2002 and forged a 274-94 record over twelve seasons. His career winning percentage of .743 puts him in Division II's top ten. His 2014 squad won the Division II national championship, and Anderson was named the Division II Coach of the Year.

He didn't give up on his dream job for several years. He applied for the MU job in 2006 and again in 2011 but was passed over both times "without serious consideration." On a local radio show in March 2014, he admitted he had finally dismissed the possibility of ever being named the head basketball coach at Missouri.

Less than a month later, Anderson was riding his bicycle when

TIGERS

he picked up a missed call. To his surprise, it was from a search firm seeking Frank Haith's successor at Missouri. Five days later, he interviewed with Athletic Director Mike Alden. A follow-up meeting with the board of curators came next.

On April 28, only nine days after he was surprised by a phone call while he was out exercising, Kim Anderson was announced as the men's head basketball coach at Missouri. He had landed his dream job.

No matter how tightly or doggedly we cling to our dreams, devotion to them won't make them a reality. Moreover, the cold truth is that all too often dreams don't come true even when we put forth a mighty effort. The realization of dreams generally results from a head-on collision of persistence and timing.

But what if our dreams don't come true because they're not the same dreams God has for us? That is, they're not good enough and, in many cases, they're not big enough.

God calls us to great achievements because God's dreams for us are greater than our dreams for ourselves. Could the Israelites, wallowing in the misery of slavery, even dream of a land of their own? Could they imagine actually going to such a place?

The fulfillment of such great dreams occurs only when our dreams and God's will for our lives are the same. Our dreams should be worthy of our best — and worthy of God's involvement in making them come true.

I wouldn't have hired me either in 1999. I wasn't ready.
— Kim Anderson on being passed over for his dream job

**If our dreams are to come true, they
must be worthy of God's involvement in them.**

YOU DECIDE

Read Acts 16:22-34.

"[The jailer] asked, 'Sirs, what must I do to be saved?'
They replied, 'Believe in the Lord Jesus, and you will be
saved'" (vv. 30-31).

Gary Pinkel's decision was so universally derided that "every-one thought [his] visor had cut off circulation to his brain." A few minutes later, the decision had all the earmarks of genius.

In the 2009 Kansas game, the Tigers trailed the Jayhawks 39-36 with three minutes left to play. With only one timeout left, they faced fourth-and-4 at their own 39. To the dismay and outrage of practically every MU fan who was paying attention, Pinkel elected to punt, turning the game over to a defense "that had been publicly depantsed for the previous 3 1/2 hours." Writer Joe Walljasper said the decision "was not a plan for victory" but a bid for Pinkel to join the unemployment line.

But punt the head Tiger did, and Jake Harry delivered with his fifth punt of the game to be downed inside the 20, this one at the Kansas 3. The Jayhawk coaching cadre then made some bad decisions of its own. Instead of running the ball and the clock, the Hawks threw two incomplete passes that burned off only ten seconds. Then senior end Brian Coulter and redshirt freshman end Aldon Smith, the Big 12 Defensive Newcomer of the Year, blew up a third-down quarterback draw with a tackle in the end zone for a safety.

TIGERS

The Tigers trailed by only one and set up shop at the Jayhawk 48 after the free kick. MU quickly moved downfield, a 27-yard run getting the Tigers to the Kansas 5-yard line. Pinkel then made a pair of good decisions, letting quarterback Blaine Gabbert take a knee twice. As the clock ticked to zero, Grant Ressel, "the kicker with the face of Opie Taylor and the nerves of a burglar," booted a 27-yard field goal for the 41-39 win.

The decisions you have made along the way have shaped your life at every pivotal moment just as Gary Pinkel's decision to punt helped decide the '09 Kansas game. Some decisions you made suddenly and carelessly; some you made carefully and deliberately; some were forced upon you. You may have discovered that some of those spur-of-the-moment decisions have turned out better than your carefully considered ones.

Of all your life's decisions, however, none is more important than one you cannot ignore: What have you done with Jesus? Even in his time, people chose to follow Jesus or to reject him, and nothing has changed. As it was with the Roman jailer, the decision must still be made and nobody can make it for you. Ignoring Jesus won't work either; that is, in fact, a decision, and neither he nor the consequences of your decision will go away.

Considered or spontaneous — how you arrive at a decision for Jesus doesn't matter; all that matters is that you get there.

I thought everybody thought it was a great decision. I thought they were cheering for me. I guess it was KU fans.
— Gary Pinkel, joking about his decision to punt

A decision for Jesus may be spontaneous or considered; what counts is that you make it.

REDEEMED

Read 1 Peter 1:17-25.

"It was not with perishable things such as silver or gold that you were redeemed from the empty way of life handed down to you from your forefathers, but with the precious blood of Christ" (vv. 18-19).

John Moseley was in dire need of some redemption. It took him eight seconds to get it.

Al Onofrio's 1973 Tigers went 7-4 and landed in the Sun Bowl against Auburn on Dec. 29. The Tigers had used a simple formula all season: Send fullback Ray Bybee and tailback Tommy Reamon at the defense until it wore down. The Sun Bowl was no different as Bybee ran for 127 yards and Reamon had 110 yards.

A rare trick play, though, propelled the Tigers into a lead they never lost. From the Auburn 35, slotback Chuck Link took a pitchout from quarterback Ray Smith, starting only his second game. Link suddenly stopped short and lofted a strike to tight end John Kelsey, who was wide open at the 5.

The Tigers scored three quick second-quarter touchdowns to lead 21-3 and pretty much knock Auburn out of contention. Except that the Tigers moved 80 yards in the waning seconds of the half for a touchdown. The score came on a fourth-and-17 play on which Moseley, an All-American kick returner and defensive back (See Devotion No. 49.), was beaten. Only 8 seconds were left in the half, and Auburn was right back in the game.

TIGERS

That surely wasn't time enough for Missouri to do anything, but Auburn must not have figured on Moseley's desire to atone for his mistake. He fielded the kickoff at his 16, cut to his left behind a wedge of blockers, and sailed up the sideline. He was running wide open when he crossed midfield, and no one could catch him.

Moseley's "pulsating gallop" broke Auburn's back and its heart. He had his redemption and MU had an easy 34-17 win.

In our capitalistic society, we know all about redemption. Just think "rebate" or store or product coupons. To receive the rebates or the discount, though, we must redeem them, cash them in.

"Redemption" is a business term; it reconciles a debt, restoring one party to favor by making amends as was the case with John Moseley and the Missouri fans in the Sun Bowl. In the Bible, a slave could obtain his freedom only upon the paying of money by a redeemer. In other words, redemption involves the cancelling of a debt the individual cannot pay on his own.

While literal, physical slavery is incomprehensible to us today, we nevertheless live much like slaves in our relationship to sin. On our own, we cannot escape from its consequence, which is death. We need a redeemer, someone to pay the debt that gives us the forgiveness from sin we cannot give ourselves.

We have such a redeemer. He is Jesus Christ, who paid our debt not with money, but with his own blood.

It was definitely the key play of the game.
— Al Onofrio on John Moseley's redemptive return

To accept Jesus Christ as your savior is to believe that his death was a selfless act of redemption.

GOOD NEWS

Read Matthew 28:1-10.

'"He has risen from the dead and is going ahead of you into Galilee. There you will see him.' Now I have told you" (v. 7).

The same week some really big news was made off the field, the Tigers made some news on the field with what they did to Texas.

On Sunday, Nov. 6, 2011, Missouri Chancellor Brady Deaton, MU Athletic Director Mike Alden, and a gaggle of SEC officials announced at a press conference that the university was joining the SEC. The groundbreaking news meant Missouri would be leaving a conference of rivals it had associated with since 1907.

Noteworthy was that Tiger football players were not on hand in the student center for the news. Their attention was on the upcoming game against Texas. "I'm not worried about the SEC," receiver T.J. Moe said. "It'll be fun for next year, but right now I'm worried about playing Texas."

Despite all the discussion, conversation, and excitement about the move swirling around them, the Tigers stayed focused on making some news themselves by beating the Longhorns for the first time since 1997 and for the first time ever under head coach Gary Pinkel. And they did just that in what one writer — interestingly enough — called "a game of SEC football."

With its punishing defense leading the way, MU "controlled the line of scrimmage, stonewalled the league's No. 1 rushing attack and perhaps allayed fears they can't trade punches in the SEC slugfests." The Longhorns managed only 76 yards rushing on 29 tries. "They wanted to run the ball. We stopped the run," said strong safety Kenji Jackson.

In a nutshell, that explained what happened. The Tigers got enough help from the offense and made news and history with a 17-5 win.

The story of mankind's "progress" through the millennia could be summarized and illustrated quite well in an account of how we disseminate our news. For much of recorded history, we told our stories through word of mouth, which required time to spread across political and geographical boundaries. That method also didn't do much to ensure accuracy.

Today, though, our news — like Missouri's move to the SEC — is instantaneous. Yesterday's news is old news; we want to see it and hear about it as it happens.

But the biggest news story in the history of the world goes virtually unnoticed every day by the so-called mainstream media. It is, in fact, often treated as nothing more than superstition. But it's true, and it is the greatest, most wonderful news of all.

What headline should be blaring from every news source in the world? This one: "Jesus Rises from Dead, Defeats Death." It's still today's news, and it's still the most important news story ever.

I really do not care about that conference. My mind right now is on these seniors and getting them a win Saturday (vs. Texas).
— Cornerback Kip Edwards on the news of MU's move to the SEC

The biggest news story in history took place
when Jesus Christ walked out of that tomb.

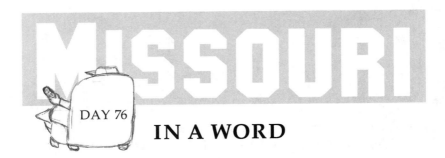

IN A WORD

Read Matthew 12:33-37.

*"For out of the overflow of the heart the mouth speaks.
The good man brings good things out of the good stored
up in him, and the evil man brings evil things out of the
evil stored up in him" (vv. 34b-35).*

Bill Roper's first words got the Missouri faithful in his corner.

After the 1908 football season, Missouri professor of Greek
W.G. Manley went East to secure a new coach. He returned to
Columbia with Roper, 29 years old and a Princeton grad who had
been coaching at his alma mater.

About 400 students greeted the new head coach at the train
station, and he needed only one sentence to have them shouting
with excitement. "I understand you want to beat Kansas," Roper
said. He was right about that. The school's oldest and most bitter
rivalry stood at an embarrassing 3-13-2 for the Tigers.

Saying the right thing was one of Roper's strengths. It served
him well in his careers as a lawyer, a politician, an insurance sales-
man, and a football coach. Described as "neither innovator nor
taskmaster," Roper relied heavily on emotion. "He was a great
psychologist," said one of his successors at Princeton.

He certainly used words as a tool. He installed what he called
walking and talking Sunday afternoons. The players and coaches
would trek eight to ten miles, talking all the way. When Missouri
met Kansas in '09 with the championship of the Missouri Valley

TIGERS

Conference on the line, Roper called each of his key players to his room the night before the game. He told them, "The alumni don't think you can beat Kansas, but I don't believe them. The team that won't be beat, can't be beat."

His methods — including his words — were effective. Missouri beat Kansas 12-6. In Roper's only season at Missouri (a much bigger paycheck took him back to Princeton), the Tigers finished 7-0-1, the only undefeated season in the school's history.

These days, everybody's got something to say and likely as not a place to say it. Talk has really become cheap as the 24-hour media scramble to fill their programming with just about anyone who is willing to expound on just about anything.

But words still have power, and that includes not just those of the talking heads, hucksters, and pundits on television, but ours also. Our words are perhaps the most powerful force we possess for good or for bad. The words we speak today can belittle, wound, humiliate, and destroy. They can also inspire, heal, protect, and create. Our words both shape and define us. They also reveal to the world the depth of our faith.

We should never make the mistake of underestimating the power of the spoken word. After all, speaking the Word was the only means Jesus had to get his message across — and look what he managed to do.

We must always watch what we say, because others sure will.

He was wonderful in talking to the team.
— Princeton football coach Charley Caldwell (1945-56) on Bill Roper

Choose your words carefully; they are the most powerful force you have for good or for bad.

STORY TIME

Read Luke 8:26-39.

*"'Return home and tell how much God has done for you.'
So the man went away and told all over town how much
Jesus had done for him" (v. 39).*

From an outfielder doing a handstand during a game to a pitcher getting a bus driver mad at him, the Tigers' national-champion baseball team of 1954 had some stories to tell.

Missouri's first national champions in a team sport went 22-4 and ripped through the Big Seven with an 11-1 record. Powered by a .311 team batting average and a 2.30 team earned run average and led by legendary coach John "Hi" Simmons, they won the College World Series by dropping only one game. Behind pitcher Ed Cook and a home run from Buddy Cox, the Tigers beat Rollins College 4-1 in the championship game.

The title is a story in itself, but so is pitcher Norm Stewart's reaction after a horrible start against Oklahoma A&M (now State). Stewart, who later coached MU men's basketball, didn't get out of the first inning. "Our team bus driver was Bob Finley, the mayor of Mexico, Mo.," Stewart said. "I was so mad I hit the side of his bus with my cleats, and then I had *him* mad at me."

Outfielder Lee Roy Wynn found himself in a real bind prior to the game against top-seeded Michigan in the world series. Simmons told him the day before that he would start. That night in the hotel, Wynn busted his glasses wrestling with pitcher Bob

TIGERS

Bauman, who was also a Mizzou fullback. Rather than miss his chance to start, Wynn didn't tell Simmons and played the game with one lens. After the 4-3 win, he confessed to Simmons. "He turned white as a ghost," Wynn remembered.

Once to relieve the boredom in the bullpen, Stewart convinced "team cutup" Bob Musgrave to do a handstand while he was playing right field against an overmatched Colorado team.

Yep, the '54 national champions have some stories to tell.

So maybe you didn't win a national title in college or even a state title in high school. You nevertheless have a story to tell; it's the story of your life and it's unique. No one else among the billions of people on this planet can tell the same story.

Part of that story is your encounter with Jesus. It's the most important chapter of all, but, strangely enough, believers in Jesus Christ often don't tell it. Otherwise brave and daring Christian men and women who wouldn't think twice of skydiving or white-water rafting often quail when they are faced with the prospect of speaking about Jesus to someone else. It's the dreaded "W" word: witness. "I just don't know what to say," they sputter.

But witnessing is nothing but telling your story. No one can refute it; no one can claim it isn't true. You don't get into some great theological debate for which you're ill prepared. You just tell the beautiful, awesome story of Jesus and you.

My fear was that at some point during the game I would stick my finger through the frame to itch my eye and give myself away.
— Lee Roy Wynn on playing with busted glasses vs. Michigan

We all have a story to tell, but the most important part of all is the chapter where we meet Jesus.

TURNAROUND

Read Acts 9:1-22.

*"All those who heard him were astonished and asked,
'Isn't he the man who raised havoc in Jerusalem among
those who call on this name?'" (v. 21)*

Missouri's football program apparently was going nowhere under Gary Pinkel. Then it all turned around on a night when everything seemed hopeless.

Early on, Pinkel seemed destined to add his name to the list of coaches fired in Columbia. "Many times the first couple years, I'd come home and tell (his wife) Vicki, 'I don't know why I did this,'" he recalled, referring to leaving Toledo for Missouri.

The 2003 season apparently marked a turnaround. The Tigers went 8-5 and landed their first bowl berth since 1998. But then came the regressive 5-6 record of 2004, and 2005 didn't look much better when Iowa State came to town on Oct. 15. The Tigers were 3-2, leaving Pinkel with a 25-28 record to show for his tenure.

The Tigers "were on the verge of a potentially season-defining setback" when the Cyclones led 24-14 in the fourth quarter. Then with just under nine minutes left, star quarterback Brad Smith, the school's all-time leader in rushing and second all-time leader in passing, was knocked out of the game by a blow to the head.

That left the Tiger season in the hands of a relatively untested freshman, Chase Daniel. He promptly completed five passes to set up Adam Crossett's 19-yard field goal with 4:44 left. He then

TIGERS

led the Tigers on an 87-yard drive that culminated in a 4-yard touchdown pass to senior wide receiver Sean Coffey with only 20 seconds to play. That forged a tie, and in overtime, Crossett's 26-yard field goal gave Mizzou a 27-24 win.

The MU program has never looked back from that turnaround game, which laid the foundation for the 76-36 record that has followed through the 2013 season.

Like the Tigers in 2005, we often look for some means or some spark we can use to turn our lives around. Oh, we may not be headed to prison or bankrupt or plagued by an addiction. Maybe we can't find a purpose to our life and are just drifting.

Still, our situation often seems untenable to us. We sink into gloom and despair, wasting our time, our emotions, and our energy by fretting about how bad things are and how they will never get better. How in the world can we turn things around?

Turn to Jesus; as the old hymn urges, trust and obey him. If it's that simple, then why hesitate? Well, it's also that complicated as Paul discovered when he experienced one of the most dramatic turnarounds in history. To surrender to Jesus is to wind up with a new life and to wind up with a new life, we have to surrender to Jesus. We have to give up control.

What's to lose? After all, if we're looking for a way to turn our lives around, we're not doing such a good job of running things. What's to gain? Life worth living, both temporal and eternal.

I mean, he did what you can't do.
  — Gary Pinkel on Chase Daniel's game that led to a turnaround

**A life in need of turning around
needs Jesus at the wheel.**

PAY YOUR RESPECTS

Read Mark 8:31-38.

"He then began to teach them that the Son of Man must suffer many things and be rejected by the elders, chief priests and teachers of the law, and that he must be killed" (v. 31).

The Tigers got so little respect before the 1968 Gator Bowl against Alabama that even the pillows of the place where they stayed said "Roll Tide!"

"Man, we are in Bama territory," realized Tiger safety Dennis Poppe during the visit to Jacksonville, Fla., to take on the Crimson Tide of Coach Bear Bryant. As Poppe recalled it, "At the pregame luncheon, Bear gets up and gets a standing ovation. . . . I don't think they thought of Missouri as a worthy opponent."

The 7-3 Tigers needed less than a minute and one play to gain all the respect they needed. On the first play from scrimmage, junior quarterback Terry McMillan took off around his right end and pitched to running back Greg Cook, who ripped off a 33-yard gain. That kicked off an 11-play, 70-yard drive that ended with McMillan scoring on a 4-yard run.

Alabama managed a touchdown to tie the game at 7, but after that the day belonged to the disrespected Tigers. Head coach Dan Devine decided to forgo passing altogether. Instead, the Tigers bulldozed the Tide, rushing for 402 yards. Cook led the way with 179 yards and a touchdown. McMillan rushed for 76 yards and three scores; he was the MVP despite not completing a pass.

Missouri's defense held Alabama to -45 yards rushing (a Gator Bowl record that still stands) and 32 yards of total offense. Poppe returned an interception for a TD. All-American Roger Wehrli, who honeymooned at the Gator Bowl, also had an interception.

Missouri won 35-10, the 25-point loss at the time the worst defeat Bryant had suffered at Alabama. The Associated Press gave the Gator Bowl champions some respect, sending them up to No. 9 in its final rankings.

Rodney Dangerfield made a good living with a comedic repertoire that was basically only countless variations on one punch line: "I don't get no respect." Dangerfield was successful because he struck a chord with his audience. Like the late comedian, we all seek a measure of respect in our lives. We want the respect, the esteem, and the regard we feel we have earned.

But more often than not we don't get it. Still, we shouldn't feel too badly; we're in good company. In the ultimate example of disrespect, Jesus — the Son of God — was treated as the worst type of criminal. He was arrested, bound, scorned, ridiculed, spit upon, tortured, condemned, and executed.

God allowed his son to undergo such treatment because of his high regard and his love for each one of us. We are respected by almighty God! Could anyone else's respect really matter?

Bear Bryant was the king down there.
— Dennis Poppe on MU's second-class status at the '68 Gator Bowl

You may not get the respect you deserve,
but at least nobody's spitting on you and
driving nails into you as they did to Jesus.

DAY 80

UNEXPECTEDLY

Read Matthew 24:36-51.

"No one knows about that day or hour, not even the angels in heaven, nor the Son, but only the Father" (v. 36).

Just about everyone knew what to expect when Mizzou hosted SMU in 1948 — and then the unexpected happened.

The Mustangs were college football's glamour team of '48, with eventual Heisman-Trophy winner Doak Walker appearing on the cover of *Life* magazine. They expected to go undefeated, and they got off to a fast start by outscoring Pittsburgh and Texas Tech 74-20 in the first two games of the season. The Tigers were 1-1 when the Mustangs galloped into Memorial Stadium on Oct. 9.

Despite the expectations of a relatively easy SMU win, a record crowd of nearly 31,000 showed up for the game. "It was a big ball game, that's for sure," declared John Kadlec, a guard on that 1948 Mizzou team who went on to become a fixture in MU athletics for more than fifty years. (See Devotion No. 42.)

Walker showed his stuff by intercepting a pass and leading the offense on a 50-yard scoring drive for a 7-0 halftime lead. In the second half, the Tigers drove 70 yards to tie it up. Guy "Bus" Entsminger, "considered by many the best Split T formation quarterback Don Faurot ever coached," ran 7 yards for the score. He would be inducted into the Missouri Hall of Fame in 1991.

As expected, the Mustangs appeared to be taking control of the game after that surprise, marching to the Tiger 10. But linebacker

TIGERS

Win Carter recovered a fumble. After a 59-yard Entsminger run and an exchange of punts, halfback Dick Braznell propelled the Tigers into a 14-7 lead with a short sweep around end.

With only four minutes to play, defensive back Loyd Brinkman intercepted a pass and ran it 49 yards to the Mustang 5. That set up Johnny Glorioso's score for a 20-7 lead. Walker scored late, but it wasn't enough. Unexpectedly, Missouri had a 20-14 win Dan Devine said was "remembered as one of the best in school history."

Just like SMU and its plans for an undefeated season, we think we've got everything figured out and under control, and then something unexpected like the Tigers happens. About the only thing we can expect from life with any certainty is the unexpected.

God is that way too, suddenly showing up to remind us he's still around. A friend who calls and tells you he's praying for you, a hug from your child or grandchild, a lone lily that blooms in your yard — unexpected moments when the divine comes crashing into our lives with such clarity that it takes our breath away and brings tears to our eyes.

But why shouldn't God do the unexpected? The only factor limiting what God can do in our lives is the paucity of our own faith. We should expect the unexpected from God, this same deity who caught everyone by surprise by unexpectedly coming to live among us as a man, and who will return when we least expect it.

Nobody expected us to win, but we got the upset.
— John Kadlec on the 1948 defeat of SMU

God continually does the unexpected,
like showing up as Jesus,
who will return unexpectedly.

FACING THE MUSIC

Read Psalm 98.

"Sing to the Lord a new song, for he has done marvelous things" (v. 1).

Mozart, Beethoven, Wagner — it takes a real high-brow group to specialize in that kind of music, right? Maybe not. Once upon a time, tunes by such composers made up the repertoire of Marching Mizzou, the university's marching band.

Marching music began at Missouri in 1885 when Lt. Enoch H. Crowder, a professor of military science and tactics, founded the first school band. He received a $125 grant to start the group, making the University of Missouri's Cadet Band one of the first university marching bands in the country. Crowder did, however, pay the first director's $25 monthly salary out of his own pocket. Twelve men "led by a spiffy drum major in headgear that resembled a fuzzy watermelon" made up the pioneering group.

The players furnished their own music, and it didn't in any way resemble what the marching band or the pep band plays today at halftime of a Tiger football game or at a basketball game. The band played classical music only and drew large crowds of onlookers for its weekly review as it excelled in military activities. On into the 1920s, the band stuck with the classics. A 1926 statement in the school yearbook explained, "The Band has always stood for the highest forms of music. It has never fostered that symbol of modernism known as jazz."

Nonetheless, Marching Mizzou inevitably changed with the times. Military marching and classical music were eventually left behind; women joined the ranks in 1958.

Big Mo — a 200+-pound drum — joined the band in 1981. The custom-made drum is one of the ten largest bass drums in the world and requires two students, one to pull it and one to beat it.

Musicians, the flag corps, twirlers, drum major, the Golden Girls, Big Mo — they're all part of the fun and pageantry that is Marching Mizzou, which today is some 300 members strong.

Maybe you can't play a lick or carry a tune in the proverbial bucket. Or perhaps you do know your way around a guitar or a keyboard and can sing "Fight Tigers!" on karaoke night without closing the joint down.

Unless you're a professional musician, however, how well you play or sing really doesn't matter. What counts is that you have music in your heart and sometimes you have to turn it loose.

Worshipping God has always included music in some form. That same boisterous and musical enthusiasm that you exhibit at Missouri's football games should be a part of the joy you have in your personal worship of God.

Take a moment to count the blessings in your life, all gifts from God. Then consider that God loves you, he always will, and he has arranged through Jesus for you to spend eternity with him. How can that song God put in your heart not burst forth?

The more noise, the more spirit.
— *Motto of MU band from 1903-10*

You call it music; others may call it noise;
sent God's way, it's called praise.

FATHERS AND SONS

Read Luke 3:1-22.

"And a voice came from heaven: 'You are my Son, whom I love; with you I am well pleased'" (v. 22).

As Corby Jones prepared to take the field to start the season, he was crying so hard he could barely breathe. That's because for the first time, his dad wasn't there with him.

For three seasons at MU, Jones and his father, Curtis, shared a pre-game ritual. The quarterback would sit on a bench in the locker room, and his dad, the Tigers' defensive line coach, would kneel in front of him. He would offer some advice, maybe speak about the weather, and then they would pray together. He would rise, wish his son "good luck," and kiss him on the head.

As the 1998 season began on Sept. 5 against Bowling Green, however, Missouri's senior quarterback was alone. There would be no weather report, no kiss on the head. And there would never be again. Less than two months before, Curtis Jones had died after suffering a massive heart attack. He was 55. "He controlled everything that he could control," said Gwen Jones about her husband and his family history of heart disease. "He could not control genetics."

In January 1995, Corby, a high school senior, told his dad, "I think I'm going to Missouri." "For a moment, Curtis sat mute, mock serious. Then he laughed for what seemed like hours."

When Curtis returned to Missouri in 1994 as an assistant coach, he had come home. He was a linebacker at Mizzou in 1966 and '67 and spent three seasons in the NFL. Now his son was headed to Columbia to eventually become one of the best quarterbacks in the country. "To have Corby with him meant so much," said Gwen. "He was ecstatic."

Only, Corby would play his last season of college ball alone.

Contemporary American society largely belittles and marginalizes fathers and their influence upon their sons. Men are perceived as necessary to effect pregnancy; after that, they can leave and everybody's better off.

But we need look in only two places to appreciate the enormity of that misconception: our jails — packed with males who lacked the influence of fathers in their lives as they grew up — and the Bible. God — being God — could have chosen any relationship he desired between Jesus and himself, including society's approach of irrelevancy. Instead, the most important relationship in all of history was that of father-son.

God obviously believes a close, loving relationship between fathers and sons, such as that of Corby Jones and his dad, is crucial. For men and women to espouse otherwise or for men to walk blithely and carelessly out of their children's lives constitutes disobedience to the divine will.

Simply put, God loves fathers. After all, he is one.

Over the years he gave me a million reminders. Now that he's not around to repeat them, I remember them better than ever.
— Corby Jones, speaking of his dad, Curtis

A model for the father-child relationship is found in that of Jesus the Son with God the Father.

STAR POWER

Read Luke 10:1-3, 17-20.

*"The Lord appointed seventy-two others and sent them
two by two ahead of him to every town and place where he
was about to go" (v. 1).*

Jim Johnson wasn't a star at Missouri. He had to wait for his
time in the NFL to become one.

Johnson had only one season, 1962, as MU's starting quarterback. "His statistics were mediocre," said one writer, and another
called him a "defensive specialist who ran much better than he
threw." In fact, Johnson attempted only 33 passes all season and
completed only twelve for a grand total of 198 yards.

What Johnson could do, though, was win. That '62 team, on
which he doubled up as a starting safety, went 8-1-2, finished at
No. 12, and beat Georgia Tech in the Bluebonnet Bowl.

MU athletics hall-of-famer John Kadlec recalled that the Tigers
"probably threw the ball eight or nine times a game back then,"
but Johnson brought the requisite toughness to the position. "You
had to be a tough guy to play quarterback in an offense like that,"
Kadlec said, "because you're going to get hit."

Johnson used that toughness to become a star in the NFL after
his brief, unremarkable career in Columbia. He didn't, however,
became a star player. Instead, he became a legendary defensive
coach, earning a reputation as a "defensive mastermind."

Johnson was an assistant with Dan Devine at Notre Dame for

seven seasons before he went to the pros. He spent 23 years in the NFL and was known for his "complicated schemes that pressured quarterbacks." When Johnson died in 2009 at age 68, one pro head coach called him "a pioneering and brilliant strategist."

In 2010, the Tiger quarterback who wasn't a star in Columbia officially became one when he was posthumously inducted into Missouri's Intercollegiate Athletics Hall of Fame.

Football teams are like other organizations in that they may have a star but the star would be nothing without the supporting cast. It's the same in a private company, in a government bureaucracy, in a military unit, and just about any other team of people with a common goal.

That includes the team known as a church. It may have its "star" in the preacher, who is — like the quarterback or the company CEO — the most visible representative of the team. Preachers are, after all, God's paid, trained professionals.

But when Jesus rounded up a team of seventy-two folks and sent them out, he didn't have any experienced evangelists or any educated seminary graduates on his payroll. All he had was a bunch of no-names who loved him. Centuries later, nothing has changed. God's church still depends on those whose only pay is the satisfaction of serving and whose only qualification is their abiding love for God. God's church needs you.

He wasn't a star, but he made a lot out of what he had.
— John Kadlec on Jim Johnson at Missouri

Yes, the church needs its professional clergy, but it also needs those who serve as volunteers because they love God; the church needs you.

STRANGE BUT TRUE

Read Philippians 2:1-11.

"And being found in appearance as a man, he humbled himself and became obedient to death – even death on a cross!" (v. 7)

Nebraska just flat-out slaughtered the Tigers in 1927. Yet, in one of the strangest games in Missouri's long history, MU won.

In the 1920s, under the leadership of head coach Gwinn Henry, Missouri's football program enjoyed a period of unprecedented prosperity and received its first real national recognition. The latter was intentional as Henry scheduled both intersectional and tougher competition to bring some attention to Columbia.

Henry was "a trim, spectacled Texan who neither smoked nor drank nor swore." Strangely enough, he was better known as a track coach; he headed up both sports at Missouri. In his eight seasons as the Tigers' head football coach (1923-31), Henry won 40 games, at the time the most ever. His strangest win was clearly the defeat of Nebraska in 1927.

After opening the season with a 13-6 win over Kansas State, Missouri hosted Nebraska on Oct. 8. Simply and quite truthfully put, the Huskers beat the daylights out of the Tigers that day. They rushed for 327 yards while Missouri managed only a dismal total of 28 yards. They had 20 first downs to MU's 5.

Nebraska scored in the opening minute of the second quarter, but Bob Byars blocked the PAT kick to keep the score at 6-0. After

TIGERS

that, the gritty, determined Tigers hung tough. Miller Brown, Bill Gibson, and Bill Smith all blocked punts (yes, three!), and Brown, Earl Diemund, and Enoch Drumm all intercepted passes.

Captain George Flamank threw a 12-yard touchdown pass to halfback Bert Clark, and Paul Maschoff kicked the extra point. After the touchdown, Flamank and Clark both limped out of the game. Nebraska spent the afternoon running all over the Tigers, except when it came time to score. That lone touchdown stood up, and Missouri held on for a strange 7-6 win.

Some things in life are so strange their existence can't really be explained. How else can we account for the sport of curling, tofu, that people go to bars hoping to meet the "right" person, the proliferation of tattoos, and the behavior of teenagers?

And how strange is God's plan to save us? Think a minute about what God did. He could have come roaring down, destroying and blasting everyone whose sinfulness offended him, which, of course, is pretty much all of us. Then he could have brushed off his hands, nodded the divine head, and left a scorched planet in his wake. All in a day's work.

Instead, God came up with a totally novel plan: He would save the world by becoming a human being, letting himself be humiliated, tortured, and killed, thus establishing a kingdom of justice and righteousness that will last forever.

It's a strange way to save the world — but it's true.

Funny thing about it, but I didn't really throw that many passes.
— George Flamank on the strange touchdown that beat Nebraska in '27

**It's strange but true: God allowed himself
to be killed on a cross to save the world.**

POP THE QUESTION

Read Matthew 16:13-17.

"'But what about you?' he asked. 'Who do you say I am?'" (v. 15)

Missouri catcher Megan Christopher had a question for her pitcher, Jana Hainey. Hainey had the perfect answer.

When Hainey was 12, she tacked a sheet of paper on the bulletin board in her room that read "6 years to the dream." The next line made the dream clear: "Mizzou softball."

A left-handed pitcher, Hainey was recruited to Missouri by Ty Singleton, who left for New Mexico after the 2006 season before she ever arrived on campus. The new coach, Ehren Earleywine, told her he couldn't promise her anything.

Hainey saw limited action as a freshman in 2007, and injuries slowed her down the next two seasons. She was 10-3 with a 2.24 ERA in 2008 and 7-0 with a 1.64 ERA as a junior but battled a bum shoulder that limited her to a spot as the team's no.-4 pitcher. With hard-throwing star Chelsea Thomas and all-conference pitcher Kristin Nottelmann on hand for 2010, Hainey entered the season penciled in as the no.-3 pitcher.

But Nottelmann struggled some and Thomas went down with an injury. Suddenly, Hainey emerged as the team's late-season ace. Thus, on Saturday night, May 15, she was the starter in the opening game of the Big 12 Tournament against Oklahoma State.

That's when Christopher, a defensive replacement, walked out

TIGERS

to the mound to pop the question. "So Jana," she said, "what's working today?" It was the sixth inning, and "Hainey was throwing the game of her life." Her dead-on answer? "You know, Megan, it's just one of those days. Everything is working."

She threw a 5-0 shutout against 14th-ranked OSU, which had swept MU in the regular season. The team went on to set a school record with 51 wins and advance to the college world series.

Life is an ongoing search for answers, and thus whether our life is lived richly or is wasted is largely determined by both the quality and the quantity of the answers we find. Life is indeed one question after another. What's for dinner? Can we afford a new car? What kind of team will Missouri have this season?

But we also continuously seek answers to questions at another, more crucial level. What will I do with my life? Why am I here? Why does God allow suffering and tragedy?

An aspect of wisdom is reconciling ourselves to and being comfortable with the reality that we will never know all of the answers. Equally wise is the realization that the answers to life's more momentous questions lie within us, not beyond us.

One question overrides all others, the one Jesus asked Peter: "Who do you say I am?" Peter gave the only correct answer: "You are the Son of the Living God." How you answer that question is really the only one that matters, since it decides not just how you spend your life but how you spend eternity.

We needed revenge. That was my mindset. Just getting them back.
— Jana Hainey, answering a question after the win over OSU

**Only one question in life determines
your eternal fate: Who do you say Jesus is?**

OF GOOD CHEER

Read Matthew 21:1-11.

"The crowds that went ahead of him and those that followed shouted" (v. 9).

It's fitting that the most famous of all University of Missouri cheers came about because of the cheerleaders.

During the 22-21 road win over Ohio State in 1976, the Tiger cheerleaders were impressed by a cheer in which the two sides of the stadium answered each other in spelling out "Ohio." "We were speechless," recalled cheerleader Jess Bushyhead, "having never thought of doing something like that before."

The long bus ride back to Columbia gave Bushyhead plenty of time to get with fellow cheerleaders Jim Henry, Steve Wendling, Marty Handy, Dottie Bellman, Amy Lissner, Anne Pobanz, Bill Irwin, Laurie Flynn, Becky Kamitsuka, and Greg Johnson. They plotted a way to do the Buckeyes one better. After some discussion, Mini-Mizzou member Cedric Lemmie piped up with the idea of shouting "M-I-Z" to be answered by "Z-O-U!" It was a winner.

The cheerleaders then set about the difficult problem of implementing the new cheer, introducing it at the next home game. As Bushyhead recalled it, the idea went "over a bit strangely" because "the crowd didn't really know what we were doing."

Rather than give up, the group decided to step up their game. At the next home game, on Oct. 16 against Iowa State, the cheerleaders went into the crowd and directed fans seated opposite the band to yell "Z-O-U" when the band yelled "M-I-Z." "Just before kickoff, we tried it," Bushyhead said. "The band yelled 'M-I-Z,' and to our astonishment, the crowd yelled back with us, 'Z-O-U.' "

But the cheerleaders wanted the entire crowd involved. They enlisted the help of the pompom girls and then spaced everyone strategically throughout the crowd to provide instructions for a massive cheer to start the second half. "We all knew it was going to work," Bushyhead said. And it did.

Chances are you go to work every day, do your job well, and then go home. You're indispensable to the nation's efficiency and your community's well-being. Even so, nobody cheers for you or waves pompoms in your face. Your name probably will never elicit a standing ovation when a PA announcer calls it.

It's just as well, since public opinion is notoriously fickle. Consider, if you will, what happened to Jesus. When he entered Jerusalem, he was the object of raucous cheering and an impromptu parade. The crowd's adulation reached such a frenzy they tore branches off trees and threw their clothes on the ground.

Five days later the crowd shouted again, only this time they screamed for Jesus' execution.

So don't worry too much about not having your personal set of cheering fans. Remember that you do have one personal cheerleader who will never stop pulling for you: God.

A bunch of creative and energetic college kids improvised and implemented a cheer that will energize Mizzou fans for generations to come.
— *Todd Donoho and Dan O'Brien in* MizzouRah!

**Just like the sports stars, you do have
a personal cheerleader: God.**

DAY 87

ANGER MANAGEMENT

Read James 1:19-27.

"Everyone should be quick to listen, slow to speak and slow to become angry, for man's anger does not bring about the righteous life that God desires" (vv. 19-20).

Tommy Saunders' grandfather got really angry with a Missouri football coach and heatedly told the assistant just how wrong he was. As it turned out, grandpa was right.

Saunders ended his career at MU in 2008 as one of the top ten receivers in Tiger history. He won the team's underclassman leadership award in 2007 and was a team captain as a senior. He started more than forty games. "He's a special guy in so many ways," praised then-wide receivers coach Andy Hill.

It was a nice thing for the assistant coach to say, since a certain member of the Saunders family didn't have many good things to say about him for a long while. Despite a stellar high-school career as a wide receiver and a defensive back, Saunders had to sell himself to Missouri. After MU's 2004 spring scrimmage, Hill led Saunders, his mother, and his grandparents on a tour of the campus and then delivered his assessment of Saunders' future in Columbia: He was welcome to join the program as a walk-on.

Saunders' maternal grandfather took issue with that idea and let Hill know it."My grandpa yelled at [Hill] for why they didn't recruit me," Saunders later recalled. "Coach Hill was really nice about it." Despite grandpa's anger, Hill didn't change his belief that Saunders was too small and too slow to rate a scholarship.

"His grandfather felt like he deserved a better opportunity," Hill said about that meeting. "And, obviously, he was exactly right." Saunders walked on and earned a scholarship in 2006.

Saunders' grandfather died of cancer in January 2008. He had long before patched up his relationship with Hill, forgiving him for not seeing what he had known all along.

Our society today is well aware of anger's destructive power because too many of us don't manage our anger as well as Tommy Saunders' grandpa did. Anger is a healthy component of a functional human being until — like other normal emotions such as fear, grief, and worry — it escalates out of control. Anger abounds around Columbia when Missouri loses; it's a natural response. The trouble comes when that anger intensifies from annoyance and disappointment to rage and destructive behavior.

Anger has both practical and spiritual consequences. Its great spiritual danger occurs when anger is "a purely selfish matter and the expression of a merely peevish vexation at unexpected and unwelcome misfortune or frustration" as when Missouri fumbles at the 5-yard line. It thus interferes with the living of the righteous, Christ-like life God intends for us.

Our own anger, therefore, can incur God's wrath; making God angry can never be anything but a perfectly horrendous idea.

[Tommy Saunders'] grandfather did not really care for me.
— Andy Hill

**Anger becomes a problem when it escalates
into rage and interferes with the righteous life
God intends for us.**

ANGER MANAGEMENT   175

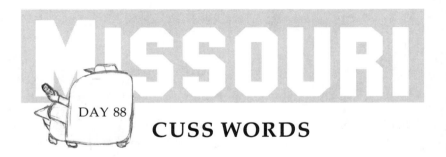

DAY 88

CUSS WORDS

Read Psalm 10.

"[The wicked man's] mouth is full of curses and lies and threats; trouble and evil are under his tongue" (v. 7).

One Missouri coach's cursing resulted in a rebellion by the players that got him fired in the middle of the season.

Thomas Kelley was the Missouri head football coach in 1922. His captain was senior Herb Bunker, who had seen only one college game when he arrived on campus in 1919. He had not played any high school football either since his school back home in Nevada, Missouri, didn't have a team. But he "was built like a blacksmith" at 6-3 and 190 pounds. He also had "the brain of an egghead, and the soul of a Sunday school teacher."

Bunker joined teammate Johnny Knight as the only Missouri athletes to letter in four sports. At tackle and center, he was a 60-minute player in football. In basketball, he was a rebounding machine who won Helms Hall of Fame recognition. He was a catcher-outfielder on the baseball team and a shotputter in track.

A gentle giant who stood tall physically and morally, Bunker was the team leader at a difficult time. As he put it, his head coach was "a raucous character who cussed and abused the squad all the time." The players stayed in a constant state of upheaval and rebellion with Bunker repeatedly talking teammates into staying rather than turning in their uniforms.

After a pair of close defeats to Kansas State and Oklahoma,

"the abuse became more venomous." Bunker determined the time had come to seek outside counsel. He turned to a local alumnus close to the program, who listened and then took the captain to the school president.

Bunker remembered the university's head man as "a Southern gentleman" who asked pertinent questions. He specifically asked if the coach had cursed and kicked a particular player. Bunker regretfully said he had. The president demanded and received the coach's immediate resignation.

We live in a coarsened culture where words no one would utter in polite society a few decades ago now spew from our music and our television sets — and our own mouths. Honestly answer these indelicate questions: With what name did you christen that slow driver you couldn't pass? What unflattering words did you have for that stubborn golf ball that wouldn't stay in the fairway? And what four-letter words do you sprinkle liberally in your conversations with people whom you want to think of you as "cool"?

Some argue that profane language is really harmless expression. It is in reality quite damaging, though, because of what its use reveals about the speaker: a lack of character, a lack of vocabulary, and a lack of respect for others and reverence for God.

The words you speak reveal what's in your heart, and what God seeks there is love and gentleness, not vileness.

American professional athletes are bilingual; they speak English and profanity.

— NHL Legend Gordie Howe

**Our words — including profane ones —
expose what's in our hearts.**

JUST PERFECT

Read Matthew 5:43-48.

"Be perfect, therefore, as your heavenly Father is perfect"
(v. 48).

The Tigers once had a perfect football season — even though they lost a game.

The 1960 Missouri team can still quite creditably support a claim to being the greatest team the school has ever had. Except for one lapse, they pretty much dominated everyone they played.

The key to Dan Devine's third season was quarterback Ron Taylor, who ran his coach's power sweep to perfection. With a five-man blocking wedge, the offense was virtually unstoppable.

And so the wins came. 20-0 over SMU, the first season opener the Tigers had won since 1947. 28-7 over Big-Eight newcomer Oklahoma State. 21-8 over a favored Penn State team. In the win, end Danny LaRose probably wrapped up his All-America honors. Before the Eastern media, he starred on defense, punted, and caught a 16-yard touchdown toss from Taylor.

Air Force was next, 34-8; K State was crushed 45-0; Iowa State fell 34-8; Nebraska was blitzed 28-0. Colorado was tough, but the Tigers pulled out a 16-6 win.

In the big showdown against Oklahoma (See Devotion No. 30.), Missouri prevailed 41-19. The AP followed up by voting the 9-0 Tigers No. 1. And then came perhaps the most heartbreaking loss in MU's long football history. A "tremendously talented Kansas team" stunned the Tigers 23-7.

The disappointed squad bounced back to whip Navy with Heisman-Trophy winner Joe Bellino 21-14 in the Orange Bowl. In the game, Norm Beal returned an interception 90 yards for a TD.

Thus, the Tigers finished 10-1, but that changed when Kansas was stripped of two wins — including Missouri's — for using an ineligible player. Technically, the Tigers finished a perfect 11-0.

Nobody's perfect; we all make mistakes every day. We botch our personal relationships; at work we seek competence, not perfection. To insist upon personal or professional perfection in our lives is to establish an impossibly high standard that will eventually destroy us physically, emotionally, and mentally.

Yet that is exactly the standard God sets for us. Our love is to be perfect, never ceasing, never failing, never qualified — just the way God loves us. And Jesus didn't limit his command to only preachers and goody-two-shoes types. All of his disciples are to be perfect as they navigate their way through the world's ambiguous definition and understanding of love.

But that's impossible! Well, not necessarily, if to love perfectly is to serve God wholeheartedly and to follow Jesus with single-minded devotion. Anyhow, in his perfect love for us, God makes allowance for our imperfect love and the consequences of it in the perfection of Jesus.

If we chase perfection, we can catch excellence.

— *Vince Lombardi*

**In his perfect love for us, God provides a way
for us to escape the consequences of our
imperfect love for him: Jesus.**

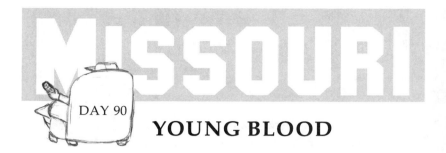

YOUNG BLOOD

Read Jeremiah 1:4-10.

*"The Lord said to me, 'Do not say, 'I am only a child' . . .
for I am with you and will rescue you" (vv. 7a, 8).*

They were called a "grab bag of 4-Fs and baby faces," but what they did "seemed like utter triumph."

By 1943, World War II had decimated athletics at MU. Basketball coach George Edwards wasn't too concerned with winning the Big Six Conference; he just wanted to field a team. Unlike Iowa State and Oklahoma, which hosted naval training units and thus could use military men, Edwards had only civilians at his disposal. These were students "too young to serve, unfit to serve or deferred from service."

So Edwards grabbed whatever he could find, and that meant a young, inexperienced lineup, not a single starter of which had ever worn a Missouri uniform before. The youngest was 17-year-old Dan Pippen, the starting center and a freshman "too young for the draft and almost too good to be true." Despite his talent, he "was literally a boy among men on most nights."

In the twilight of his 20-year career as Mizzou's head coach, Edwards pulled off one of his best coaching jobs amid the chaos that engulfed the program. With military men at their disposal, Iowa State and Oklahoma tied for the league title at 9-1. Mizzou and Kansas wound up third at 5-5. Two wins over Kansas established the Tigers as the undisputed champions of the Big Six civilians. Given the dire circumstances, MU's overall record of 9-8 was a remarkable achievement. Still greater glory lay in wait for this young team.

War played havoc with the NCAA Tournament. Especially was this true with finding a representative from the Big Six. Because navy regulations restricted the time trainees could be away from the base, both Oklahoma and Iowa State declined invitations. The NCAA turned to Missouri, which accepted the bid.

Thus, the 1943-44 squad of youngsters and novices became the first Missouri team ever to play in the NCAA Tournament.

While our media do seem obsessed with youth, most aspects of our society value experience and some hard-won battle scars. Life usually requires us to spend time on the bench as a reserve, waiting for our chance to play with the big boys and girls. You entered college as a freshman. You started out in your career at an entry-level position.

Paying your dues is traditional, but that should never stop you from doing something bold and daring right away. Nowhere is this more true than in your faith life.

You may assert that you are too young and too inexperienced to really do anything worthwhile for God. Those are just excuses, however, and God won't pay a lick of attention to them when he issues a call.

After all, the younger you are, the more time you have to serve.

Edwards's innocents were baptized by fire.
— *Writer Michael Atchison on the 1943-44 Tigers*

**Youth is no excuse for not serving God;
it just gives you more time.**

PROVE IT

Read Matthew 3.

"But John tried to deter him, saying, 'I need to be baptized by you, and do you come to me?"' (v. 14)

The snide remarks were still there almost two full seasons in, the ones that said Missouri didn't belong in the storied SEC. On a chilly night in November, the Tigers proved they not only belonged in the league, but they were one of its best.

In the summer of 2013, the pundits declared the Tigers "didn't seem to belong with their new peers." They were "a finesse team whose fancy Big 12 ways wouldn't work" in this new league. So they picked MU to finish sixth in the seven-team SEC East.

On Nov. 23, the Tigers proved the naysayers wrong, when they whipped Ole Miss 24-10 in Oxford. It wasn't the biggest win of the season; it can be argued the defeat of Georgia in Athens was. (See Devotion No. 57.) It wasn't a win that clinched a championship; that came a week later against Texas A&M. At this point of the season, the 9-1 Tigers were *expected* to whip Ole Miss. It was the way they did it that proved once and for all that they belonged.

They bullied the Rebels, pushed them around, both on offense and on defense. Twice Ole Miss had first-and-goal and didn't score a single point.

One of the most storied drives in Missouri history came with 8:08 on the clock and the 24-10 lead. Ole Miss knew what was coming and it didn't matter. Thirteen straight times the Tigers ran the ball behind linemen Justin Britt, Max Copeland, Evan Boehm, Connor McGovern, and Mitch Morse. Finally, quarterback James Franklin took a knee twice to run out the final few seconds.

What the Tigers did against the Rebels not only proved they belonged in the SEC but that they belonged in the SEC's championship game.

Like the Tigers, you, too, have to prove yourself over and over again in your life. To your teachers, to that guy you'd like to date, to your parents, to your bosses, to the loan officer. It's always the same question: "Am I good enough?" Practically everything we do in life is aimed at proving that we are.

And yet, when it comes down to the most crucial situation in our lives, the answer is always a decisive and resounding "No!" Are we good enough to measure up to God? To deserve our salvation? John the Baptist knew he wasn't, and he was not only Jesus' relative but God's hand-chosen prophet. If he wasn't good enough, what chance do we have?

The notion that only "good" people can be church members is a perversion of Jesus' entire ministry. Nobody is good enough — without Jesus. Everybody is good enough — with Jesus. That's not because of anything we have done for God, but because of what he has done for us. We have nothing to prove to God.

What they are is a very SEC team, one that invades opposing towns with an army of fans and wins games in the trenches.
— Writer Joe Walljasper on what MU proved against Ole Miss

**The bad news is we can't prove
to God's satisfaction how good we are; the good
news is that because of Jesus we don't have to.**

WORK ETHIC

Read Matthew 9:35-38.

"Then he said to his disciples, 'The harvest is plentiful but the workers are few. Ask the Lord of the harvest, therefore, to send out workers into his harvest field'" (vv. 37-38).

Brock Olivo worked so hard getting ready that for him football games were what he called "a glorified workout."

In 1997, his senior year, Olivo received the Mosi Tatupu Special Teams Player of the Year Award, the first Missouri football player to earn a national honor. He wasn't, however, just the country's best special teams player; he was also the Tigers' starting tailback. When he finished in Columbia, he was the school's all-time career leader in rushing yards (3,026), rushing touchdowns (27), and all-purpose yards (3,475), all records subsequently broken.

Along the way to having his jersey number 27 retired in 2003, Olivo won three team Offensive MVP awards, three Don Faurot Most Inspirational Player awards, and a team Special Teams MVP award. He was the Big Eight Offensive Freshman of the Year and a two-time honorable mention all-Big Eight selection.

His accolades and honors and his success on the field resulted from a workload that became part of Olivo's legend at Missouri. "Game day was easy for me," he said, "because of what I put myself through in the offseason."

When Olivo found a hill in Columbia in the summer of '95, he was so excited he rushed to tell his roommate, fullback Ron Janes, about "my wonderful discovery. . . . He looked at me as if I'd gone mad." Running the hill — described by Olivo as "so steep that you could stand at the bottom and reach out with your hand and almost touch it" — became part of his training regimen. Once the Mizzou training staff found out about it, they incorporated the hill and its rigors into the team's summer workouts. The players often grunted a sarcastic and sincere "Thanks a lot, Olivo."

The coaches required the players to attend only one of the two daily preseason running sessions, but Olivo always ran them both. "I was not the fastest or the biggest or the strongest," Olivo said, but his hard work gave him the edge he needed.

Do you embrace hard work or try to avoid it? No matter how hard you may try, you really can't escape hard work. Funny thing about all these labor-saving devices like cell phones and laptop computers: You're working longer and harder than ever. For many of us, our work defines us perhaps more than any other aspect of our lives. But there's a workforce you're a part of that doesn't show up in any Labor Department statistics or any IRS records.

You're part of God's staff; God has a specific job that only you can do for him. It's often referred to as a "calling," but it amounts to your serving God where there is a need in the way that best suits your God-given abilities and talents.

You should stand ready to work for God all the time, 24-7. Those are awful hours, but the benefits are out of this world.

I made my legacy off the football field in preparation for game day.
— Brock Olivo on his work getting ready for games

God calls you to work for him; whether
you're a worker or a malingerer is up to you.

DAY 93

THE PANIC BUTTON

Read Mark 4:35-41.

"He said to his disciples, 'Why are you so afraid? Do you still have no faith?'" (v. 40)

Missouri teams never panic and never will." So declared Dan Devine. Still, considering what was happening out on the field, it would have been a very good time to set a precedent.

Big Eight commissioner Wayne Duke called the Missouri-K State shootout of Nov. 1, 1969, the league's "most exciting [game] ever." With scouts from five bowls looking on, Missouri rolled to a comfortable 21-6 lead at halftime. Even after the Wildcats hit a bomb for a third-quarter score, Jon Staggers returned the kickoff 99 yards to keep the Tigers ahead 28-12.

Then in the space of seven seconds late in the third quarter, State scored twice. The Wildcats drove 80 yards for a score, pulled off an onside kickoff when the kicker pretended to tie his shoelace, and then scored on the first play after the kick.

It got worse. The Tigers had to punt, and K-State ripped off 80 yards in four plays to lead 31-28. Missouri still had 12 minutes to play, but clearly all those bowl scouts were as shocked as the Missouri faithful were.

Devine looked back to that moment when he issued his edict after the game about the Tigers never panicking. He was right; they didn't. Instead, quarterback Terry McMillan hooked up with wide receiver John Henley for a bomb to the Wildcat 16. After a pass to Staggers to the 1, fullback Ron McBride bulled his way in.

The Tiger defense held after the kickoff, and Staggers took the punt 40 yards to the 5. McMillan rolled out for a TD on fourth down and a 41-31 lead that held up for the 41-38 win.

The panic-free Tigers finished the season with a 9-1 record, a national ranking of No. 5, and a berth in the Orange Bowl.

Have you ever experienced that suffocating sensation of fear escalating into full-blown panic? Maybe it was the awful time when you couldn't find your child at the mall or at the beach. Or the heartstopping moment when you realized that the vehicle speeding right toward you wasn't going to be able to stop.

As the story of the disciples and the storm illustrates, the problem with panic is that it debilitates us. While some of the men in the boat were landlubbers unaccustomed to bad weather on the water, the storm panicked even the professional fishermen into helplessness. All they could do was wake up an exhausted Jesus.

We shouldn't be too hard on them, though, because we often make an even more grievous mistake. They panicked and turned to Jesus; we panic and often turn away from Jesus by underestimating both his power and his ability to handle our crises.

We have a choice when fear clutches us: We can assume Jesus no longer cares for us, surrender to it, and descend into panic, or we can remember how much Jesus loves us and resist fear and panic by trusting in him.

Remember, never panic and always maintain your dignity.
— Legendary Oklahoma football coach Bud Wilkinson

To plunge into panic is to believe that Jesus is incapable of handling the crises in our lives.

THE PANIC BUTTON   187

GOOD-BYE

Read John 13:33-38.

"My children, I will be with you only a little longer" (v. 33a).

Jeremy Maclin chose to tell Missouri good-bye, but he certainly wasn't overjoyed about it.

After a redshirt season, Maclin was a wide receiver and punt and kickoff return specialist for the Tigers in 2007 and '08. He was first-team All-America both seasons. In 2008, he led all of major-college football with 202 all-purpose yards per game. In his two seasons, he set eighteen Missouri records, including the mark for career all-purpose yards with 5,609. In 2008, he set MU records for receptions (102), receiving yards (1,260), and touchdown catches (13) in a season.

After the 2008 season ended, Maclin had to decide whether or not to enter the NFL draft. When the league informed him he was projected as a first-round pick, his decision seemed certain. Still, saying good-bye didn't come easy for Maclin. "I was kind of going back and forth," he said. "It was a long process."

The night before the deadline to declare his intentions, Maclin stayed in St. Louis with his surrogate parents. Assistant coach Cornell Ford, who had recruited him, paid a visit. Maclin didn't make his decision until the next morning after discussions with head coach Gary Pinkel and wide receivers coach Andy Hill.

The difficulty of the decision to say good-bye was apparent at the press conference that morning, Jan. 8. Maclin's lip quivered and tears rolled down his cheeks as he officially announced his decision to leave. He managed to take a few questions before he broke down, and Pinkel had to take over the microphone.

"It's been very emotional," Maclin said in stating the obvious. "This is my family. This is where I belong." But even Pinkel agreed it was time for him to go.

You've stood on the curb and watched someone you love drive off, or you've grabbed a last-minute hug before a plane leaves. Maybe it was a child leaving home for the first time or your best friends moving halfway across the country. It's an extended — maybe even a permanent — separation, and, as it did with Jeremy Maclin, good-byes hurt.

Jesus felt the pain of parting too. Throughout his brief ministry, Jesus had been surrounded by and had depended upon his friends and confidants, the disciples. About to leave them, he gathered them for a going-away supper and gave them a heads-up about what was about to happen. In the process, he offered them words of comfort. What a wonderful friend he was! Even though he was the one who was about to suffer unimaginable agony, Jesus' concern was for the pain his friends would feel.

But Jesus wasn't just saying good-bye. He was on his mission of providing the way through which none of us would ever have to say good-bye again.

I'm leaving a family. All those guys are like father figures to me.
— Jeremy Maclin on the difficulty of saying good-bye to MU

Through Jesus, we will see the day
when we say good-bye to good-byes.

NOTES
(by Devotion Day Number)

1   a group of UM students . . . darned thing blew up crooked.": Bob Broeg, *Ol' Mizzou: A Story of Missouri Football* (Huntsville, AL: The Strode Publishers, 1974), p. 15.

1   Austin L. McRae, an assistant professor . . . a team of students.: Broeg, p. 18.

1   Eleven players, a couple of . . . rode the train to St. Louis: Broeg, p. 18.

1   even stole their black- . . . sent to St. Louis instead.: Broeg, pp. 19-20.

1   Many of the student body . . . they considered huge comedy.: Broeg, p. 18.

2   a resurrection that "lift[ed] a previously dead program: Pat Forde, "Molded by His Mentor," *Yahoo Sports*, Nov. 29, 2013, http://sports.yahoo.com/news/ncaaf- -molded-by-his-mentor--gary-pinkel-has-pushed-missouri-into-prime-time-in- sec-154705507.html.

2   "started some chirping among . . . turned into howling in 2012": Forde, "Molded by His Mentor."

2   "Everyone wanted to change . . . and what we're doing.": Forde, "Molded by His Mentor."

2   The splits of the offensive . . . scaled back August conditioning.: Forde, "Molded by His Mentor."

2   We didn't come in and start changing everything.: Forde, "Molded by His Mentor."

3   the volleyball heaven of . . . became a local celebrity.: Marek Makowski, "For Molly Kreklow, Home and the Road," *The Maneater*, Sept. 10, 2013, http://www.theman eater.com/stories/2013/9/10/molly-kreklow-home-and-road/.

3   her uncle decided not to . . . to do just that.: Tod Palmer, "Senior Molly Kreklow Helps MU Volleyball," *The Kansas City Star*, Nov. 21, 2013, http://www.kansascity. com/2013/11/21/4640232/senior-molly-kreklow-helps-mu.html.

3   *Volleyball America* called her . . . the court this season.": "Kreklow, Henning Named Volleyball Magazine All-Americans," *MIZZOU TIGERS*, Jan. 20, 2014, http://www. mutigers.com/sports-w-volley/spec-rel/012014aaa.html.

3   They pressured me a . . . to go there anymore.': Palmer, "Senior Molly Kreklow Helps MU Volleyball."

4   "The MU offense was anemic,": Steve Richardson, *"Then Pinkel Said to Smith . . ."* (Chicago: Triumph Books, 2008), p. 36.

4   breaking some bones two . . . we can generate some offense.": Richardson, pp. 36-37.

4   As Snowden recalled it, the . . . his head on the sidelines,": Richardson, p. 37.

4   A golden period was about to begin: Richardson, p. 37.

5   they rated Notre Dame . . . quit taking bets on it.: Todd Donoho and Dan O'Brien, "Al's Well That Ends Well," *MizzouRah!* (Virginia Beach, Va.: The Donning Company Publishers, 2004), p. 67.

5   "The ball was just as wet on both sides,": Donoho and O'Brien, p. 69.

5   Even the heavens wept . . . 1972 college football season.: Donoho and O'Brien, p. 67.

6   The Razorbacks frequently dropped as many as nine players into pass coverage.: Graham Watson, "In Cotton Bowl, Tigers Run Hog Wild," *Mizzou-RAH!*, p. 67.

6   rendering McFadden and Jones "almost irrelevant for much of the contest.": Watson, "In Cotton Bowl," p. 64.

6   24 of which came against Missouri reserves.: Watson, "In Cotton Bowl," p. 64.

6   all those retreating defenders "gave Temple what seemed like miles to roam.": Watson, "In Cotton Bowl," p. 67.

6   We took what they gave us in this game.: Watson, "In Cotton Bowl," p. 65.

7   They gave up only 19 . . . than they did earned runs.: "Mizzou's Greatest, #82," *Rock M Nation*, May 24, 2013, www.rockmnation.com/2013/5/24/4362100/1964-missouri- baseball-hi-simmons/.

7   a scratch hit in the eighth inning.: "Mizzou's Greatest, #82."

7   leading to four unearned . . . the final game.: "Mizzou's Greatest, #82."

7   The 1964 pitching squad is . . . ever in Missouri history.: "Mizzou's Greatest, #82."

8   "I told [Jones] in the . . . was going to be there,": Donoho and O'Brien, p. 125.

8   The quarterback had four . . . at the 2-yard line.: Donoho and O'Brien, p. 125.

8   When you run trick . . . folks question your sanity.: Jim & Julie S. Bettinger, *The Book of Bowden* (Nashville: TowleHouse Publishing, 2001), p. 32

9   the City of Los Angeles invited . . . visited San Francisco and Catalina.: Broeg, p. 82.

9   they toured the Grand Canyon . . . masquerade ball in Arizona.: Broeg, p. 83.

9   A movie studio had paid a . . . shifting nervously over the delay.": Broeg, pp. 83-84.

9   The weeklong trip was a gasser.: Broeg, p. 83.

10 Fifteen minutes of fireworks.: Bill Coats, "At Last!" *Mizzou-RAH!*, p. 68.

10 "Everyone fought . . . everyone.": Coats, "At Last!" *Mizzou-RAH!*, p. 71.

10 "But instead of wilting, Mizzou untapped a reservoir of resolve.": Coats, "At Last!" *Mizzou-RAH!*, p. 71.

10 "the big gathering was in a frenzy.": Coats, "At Last!" *Mizzou-RAH!*, p. 71.

10 "the celebration that had been on hold for 25 years finally began.": Coats, "At Last!" *Mizzou-RAH!*, p. 71.

10 It hasn't sunk in, really, Pretty amazing.: Coats, "At Last!" *Mizzou-RAH!*, pp. 68, 70.

11 Not a single traffic light and only one restaurant.: Ross Dellenger, "Eye Climbing Closer to MU, NCAA Marks," *Columbia Daily Tribune*, Feb. 10, 2013, http://www.columbiatribune.com/sports/mu_basketball/eye-climbing-closer-to-mu-ncaa-marks/article.

11 "Population: 384," . . . and didn't play AAU ball.: Dellenger, "Eye Climbing Closer."

11 Instead of stepping . . . ball in the ocean.": Dellenger, "Eye Climbing Closer."

11 She's a sweet-talking country . . . lights and one restaurant.: Dellenger, "Eye Climbing Closer."

12 "I wasn't a nice guy to be around,": Dave Matter, "All Now Bright for Fisher," *Columbia Daily Tribune*, Dec. 18, 2011, http://www.columbiatribune.com/sports/mu_football/all-npw-bright-for-fisher-after-devastating-injury/article.

12 They "ask me, 'What . . . even tell us about.": Dave Matter, "The Old Man and the Knee," *Columbia Daily Tribune*, March 7, 2012, http://www.columbiatribune.com/sports/mu_football/the-old-man-and-the-knee/article.

12 "With Elvis back . . . [it's] a huge help for us,": Matter, "The Old Man."

12 I've gotten old man . . . I've been bald forever.: Matter, "The Old Man."

13 Moore "seemed destined to . . . the sixth grade twice.: Vahe Gregorian, "Once Lost, Now Found: William Moore," *Mizzou-RAH!*, p. 105.

13 His mother put him . . . offenders for a year.: Gregorian, *Mizzou-RAH!*, pp. 105-06.

13 After being released from . . . himself in constructive ones.: Gregorian, *Mizzou-RAH!*, p. 109.

13 "He began to do so . . . to cling to him,": Gregorian, *Mizzou-RAH!*, p. 110.

13 "They said he'd never . . . be in the penitentiary.": Gregorian, *Mizzou-RAH!*, p. 111.

13 He was around so much . . . fall into the shadows.: Gregorian, *Mizzou-RAH!*, p. 105.

14 he came to the U.S. in . . . brother who coached at Wisconsin.: Broeg, p. 29.

14 He once punted 110 yards . . . and with a heavy ball.": Broeg, p. 29.

14 he returned a kickoff 90 . . . four field goal in that game.: Brian C. Peterson, *Stadium Stories: Missouri Tigers* (Guilford, Conn.: The Globe Pequot Press, 2005), p. 23.

14 one of the Bears finally had . . . "Game called on account of lost ball.": Broeg, p. 31.

14 He began a law practice . . . he had changed his name: Broeg, p. 31.

14 Apparently, O'Dea had just . . . being a football celebrity.: Peterson, p. 23.

15 "Missouri seemingly found its . . . dropped below the poverty line": Joe Walljasper, "Plenty of Credit to Go Around," *Missouri Daily Tribune*, Oct. 26, 2009, http://www.columbiatribune.com/sports/plenty-of-

credit-to-go-around/article.

15   After the '06 season, . . . instead of a defender.: Walljasper, "Plenty of Credit."

15   the trophy Blitz held . . . team's first-ever soccer title.: Walljasper, "Plenty of Credit."

15   Dude, remember where we were freshman year?: David Briggs, "They've Come a Long Way, Baby," *Columbia Daily Tribune*, Oct. 26, 2009, http://www.columbiatribune. com/sports/mu/they-ve-come-a-long-way-baby/article.

16   Gary Pinkel called it Maty Mauk's final exam of the fall semester: Joe Walljasper, "Mauk Aces Final Exam," *Columbia Daily Tribune*, Nov. 10, 2013, http://www. columbiatribune.com/sports.mu_football/maulk-aces-final-exam-as-missouri-starter/article.

16   "was thrust into the . . . seat-of-his-pants crash landing": Walljasper, "Mauk Aces Final Exam."

16   The MU coaches had anticipated . . .would have to beat them.: Walljasper, "Mauk Aces Final Exam."

16   Big picture, [Maty Mauk's] 30-day trial was a major success.: Walljasper, "Mauk Aces Final Exam."

17   If Dan Devine lacked a . . . have come to Missouri.": Broeg, p. 234.

17   AD Don Faurot recalled a . . . from Tempe, Az., for a visit.: Broeg, p. 234.

17   During the flight, a . . . he was doing there.: Broeg, p. 235.

17   They rested a bit at the . . . to see my family again.": Broeg, p. 235.

17   There I sat in the dark . . . Missouri in the first place.: Broeg, p. 235.

18   knowing he would play behind . . . pro quarterback than Daniel would.: Matthew Schur, "Former MU Quarterback Chase Patton Is Chasing a New Dream," *VOX Magazine*, Sept. 1, 2011, archive.voxmagazine.com/stories/2011/09/01/former-mu-quarterback-chase-patton-is-chasing-new-dream/.

18   He's not a quitter. He's a great person, a great kid.: Dave Matter, "Happy at Home," *Columbia Daily Tribune*, April 19, 2008, http://www.columbia.tribune.com/sports/ happy-at-home/article.

19   The morning of the game . . . Broeg laughed in response.: Broeg, pp. 140-41.

19   At the break, Broeg spread . . . too good to keep,": Broeg, p. 141.

19   Years later, Christman would . . . have said those things?": Broeg, p. 141.

19   The Merry Magician called his shot.: Broeg, p. 141.

20   "proceeded to become a defensive presence of nearly mythic proportions.": Michael Atchison, *True Sons* (Virginia Beach, Va.: The Donning Company Publishers, 2006), p. 40.

20   Missouri's athletic committee challenged . . . wait until next year.: Atchison, p. 46.

20   In 1936, the Helms . . . Kansas 1922's mythical champion.: Atchison, p. 46.

20   historian Patrick Premo researched . . . Tigers to be 1922's best.: Atchison, p. 47.

20   Some deemed KU's explanation an 'alibi.': Atchison, p. 46.

21   "The people of central Missouri . . . county to county.": "Missouri Civil War Sesqui-centennial: William T. 'Bloody Bill' Anderson," http://mocivilwar150.com/history/ figure/210.

21   After a massacre and . . . man in the county.: Broeg, p. 12.

21   They called themselves the . . . grim and bloody year.": Rudi Keller, "Anniversary Approaches for Origin of MU Tiger Nickname," *Columbia Daily Tribune*, July 6, 2014, http://www.columbiatribune.com/news/civil_war/anniversary-approaches-for-origin-of-mu-tiger-nickname/article.

21   The Tigers built a . . . women and children.: Broeg, pp. 12-13.

21   The Tigers never left . . . standing picket.": Keller, "Anniversary Approaches."

21   They could hardly be . . . fitness of terms.: Keller, "Anniversary Approaches."

22   which boasted a population . . . wasn't very sophisticated,": Broeg, p. 296.

22   he set his sights on . . . as a defensive back.: "College Days: Roger Wehrli," *profoot ballhof.com*, http://www.profootballhoff.com/story/2013/12/5/college-days-roger-

wehrli/.

22   Missouri gave its last football scholarship in 1965 to Wehrli: Broeg, p. 296.

22   with the stipulation that . . . was an instant hit.": "College Days: Roger Wehrli."

22   "senior season was one for the ages.": "College Days: Roger Wehrli."

22   I felt I was through . . . and I regretted that.: "College Days: Roger Wehrli."

23   "I still had a dream of . . . something worthwhile there.": Bo Carter, "From the Diving Board to 90,000-Seat Football Stadiums," *National Football Foundation,* Nov. 9, 2008, http://www.footballfoundation.org/tabid/567/article/51840.

23   "I really had to give up what I loved,": Carter, "From the Diving Board."

23   "He works very hard at it,": R.B. Fallstrom, "Mr. Perfect," *Lubbock Avalanche-Journal,* Nov. 30, 2007, lubbockonline.com/stories/113007/col_113007012.shtml.

23   I went 1 for 2 . . . Season over.: Carter, "From the Diving Board."

24   trainer Rex Sharp called "the worst knee injury in athletics I've ever seen.": Ross Dellenger, "Josey Says He Has 'Good Chance' to Play in 2012," *Columbia Daily Tribune,* Aug. 3, 2012, http://www.columbiatribune.com/sports/mu_football/josey-says-he-has-good-chance-to-play-in/article.

24   admitted his knee injury . . . decision to turn pro,: Dave Matter, "Knee Injury Shapes Josey's Decision," *St. Louis Post-Dispatch,* Jan. 8, 2014, http://www.stltoday.com/sports/college/mizzou/knee-injury-shapes-josey-s-decision-to-entger-draft/article.

24   You always want to go out when you're on top.: Matter, "Knee Injury Shapes Josey's Decision."

25   Shire began tumbling when . . . to a gymnastics club.: Ryan Gavin, "Gymnast's Long Journey," *Mizzou Wire,* May 5, 2010, http://mizzouwire.missouri.edu/stories/2010/sarah-shire/index.php.

25   she realized that "gymnastics" . . . lit that fire again,": Gavin, "Gymnast's Long Journey."

25   in 2010 Missouri "earned . . . us in a new league": Gavin, "Gymnast's Long Journey."

25   They welcomed me with open arms.: Gavin, "Gymnast's Long Journey."

26   cold rain forced Mizzou and . . . combining for thirty-five kicks.: Broeg, p. 69.

26   he mishandled the snap when . . . would have none of it.: Broeg, p. 69.

26   Heavy rain turned Kansas State's . . . less than two minutes to play.; Broeg, p. 69.

26   Head coach Gwinn Henry sent star . . . Bond did.: Broeg, p. 70.

26   Missouri's tactic led to the . . . to also give up possession.: Broeg, p. 70.

27   the head coach "didn't dedicate . . . did not have many plays.": Richardson, p. 32.

27   "Nebraska wasn't a great team.": Richardson, p. 32.

27   "I started calling plays in . . . are going to do this.": Richardson, p. 32.

27   "a pretty good run": Richardson, p. 32.

27   "Not a word was said by any coach,": Richardson, p. 32.

27   I was worried about it. . . . . like calling your own plays.": Richardson, p. 32.

28   guard Zaire Taylor doing at . . . every second he had.: Joe Walljasper, "Mr. Big Shot Strikes Again for Missouri," *Columbia Daily Tribune,* Feb. 10, 2009, http://www.columbiatribune.com/sports/mu_basketball/mr-big-shot-strikes-again-for-missouri/article.

28   "everything is more important when the opponent is Kansas.: Walljasper, "Mr. Big Shot Strikes."

28   "with a roaring crowd . . . Tigers in their shorts,": Walljasper, "Mr. Big Shot Strikes."

28   The shot hit the rim . . . in slow motion through the hoop: Walljasper, "Mr. Big Shot Strikes."

28   He was interviewed . . . anything you're saying.": Walljasper, "Mr. Big Shot Strikes."

28   I have to have a tooth pulled.: Walljasper, "Mr. Big Shot Strikes."

29   "what could have been . . . into a gut check": "Wolfert's 34-Yard Field Goal Helps Missouri," *ESPN,* Nov. 1, 2008, scores.espn.go.com/net/recap?gameId=283060239.

29	"It was a tremendous game,": "Wolfert's 34-Yard Field Goal."
29	We found a way to win at the end when we had to.: "Wolfert's 34-Yard Field Goal."
30	After the game, the head . . . we'll beat Oklahoma.": Broeg, p. 243.
30	the nation's top-ranked defense against the rush.: Broeg, p. 254.
30	On the fourth play, . . . had yielded all season.; Broeg, p. 254.
30	Bill Callahan wrote in the . . . inherited the earth today.": Broen, p. 255.
30	A bold promise, indeed.: Broeg, p. 243.
31	He called on Mizzou alums . . . off the field on their shoulders.: Peterson, p. 8.
31	That 1911 game raised . . . the school's athletic facilities: Peterson, p. 9.
32	In 2006, he received a . . . a pretty good coach.": Marcus Wilkins, "Flamethrower," *MIZZOU Magazine*, Feb. 13, 2013, https://mizzoumag.missouri.edu/2013/02/flame thrower/.
32	I'm banging this . . . get it to vibrate).: Wilkins, "Flamethrower."
33	Simpson had only three . . . because of travel restrictions.: Broeg, p. 172.
33	The latter had received . . . than return to Clemson.: Broeg, p. 174.
33	At a rally the night . . .weapon" against the Jayhawks.: Broeg, p. 174.
33	A "tackle of unusual . . . off a 32-yard gallop.: Broeg, p. 174.
33	The big boy was just too hard for Kansas to stop.: Broeg, p. 175.
34	Missouri starting quarterback . . . strong running game.: Donoho and O'Brien, "Trojans Fed to Tigers at Coliseum," *MizzouRah!*, p. 83.
34	A large group of . . . o'clock Sunday morning.: Donoho and O'Brien, p. 84.
34	The eighth-ranked Trojans were . . . and a vaunted running game.: Donoho and O'Brien, p. 83.
35	"We still like this guy, "Pinkel said. "This guy's good enough.": Vahe Gregorian, "Mizzou's Leading Man," *Mizzou-RAH!*, p. 92.
35	informing them that the staff . . . in with my pump shotgun, Gregorian, "Mizzou's Leading Man," p. 84.
35	When Eberflus made a . . . the guy with the shotgun?": Gregorian, "Mizzou's Leading Man," p. 93.
35	The part about the . . . I may have smiled.: Gregorian, "Mizzou's Leading Man," p. 86.
36	"the least impressive 5-1 team in history": Atchison, p. 234.
36	The senior guard hadn't . . . a badly sprained ankle.: Atchison, p. 235.
36	We had the wounded in . . . would have been next.: Atchison, p. 235.
37	"one of the most innovative coaches in NCAA history.": Peterson, p. 35.
37	While their fans stormed . . . "the sunset on their shoulders.": Peterson, p. 95.
37	Don Faurot *was* the University of Missouri.: Peterson, p. 34.
38	"the bane of Mizzou's existence.": Tom Timmerman, "Breakthrough," *Mizzou-RAH!*, p. 57.
38	"If you want to . . . win games like this.": Timmerman, "Breakthrough," *Mizzou-RAH!*, p. 57.
38	"years of frustration and . . . college football's big boys.": Timmerman, "Breakthrough," *Mizzou-RAH!*, p. 53.
38	"This isn't a national . . . for our football program,": Timmerman, "Breakthrough," *Mizzou-RAH!*, p. 54..
38	who stormed the field . . . euphoric sea of gold.: Timmerman, "Breakthrough," *Mizzou-RAH!*, p. 54.
38	Mizzou stepped up and showed how good it really is.: Timmerman, "Breakthrough," *Mizzou-RAH!*, p. 53.
39	offensive coordinator Josh Henson . . . to gain 2 yards.: David Morrison, "Josey TD Sends Missouri to SEC East Title," *Columbia Daily Tribune*, Nov. 30, 2013, http://www.columbiatribune.com/sports/josey-td-sends-missouri-to-sec-east-title-in-win/article.

39 "hit the line, cut . . . not happen to happen.": Morrison, "Josey TD."

39 A big hole open and I took it.: "No. 5 Missouri Wins SEC East," *Sports Illustrated*, Nov. 30, 2013, http://sportsillustrated.cnn.com/football/ncaa/gameflash/2013/11/30/52600/index.html.

40 More amazing than the Mets!": Donoho and O'Brien, "Brown Out," *MizzouRah!*, p. 55.

40 Offensive tackle Mike Carroll . . . men of little faith.": Donoho and O'Brien, p. 55.

40 When Gray drew double . . . wide receiver John Henley.: Donoho and O'Brien, p. 55.

40 More amazing than the Mets, more discouraging . . . Majesty and Raquel Welch.: Donoho and O'Brien, p. 55.

41 He dreamed, however, of . . . like him in my path.": Ryan Gavin, "Mark of a Champion," *Mizzou Wire*, April 28, 2009, http://mizzouwire.missouri.edu/stories/2009/mark-champion/index.php.

41 Man, I'm one of those crazies. I miss that.: Gavin, "Mark of a Champion."

42 With no training table, . . . granddaddy of upset stomachs.": Broeg, p. 198.

42 Two days before the . . . do it for one year.: "John Kadlec Retires," *MIZZOU TIGERS*, Jan. 31, 2011, http://www.mutigers.com/sports/m-footbl/spec-rel/013111aaa.html.

42 I said I'd do it for one game to help out a friend.: "John Kadlec Retires."

43 "a great story of perseverance and determination,": "Max Copeland," *MIZZOU TIGERS*, http://www.mutigers.com/sports/m-footbl/mtt/max_copeland_465234.html.

43 He was regarded as . . . and then keep working,": Joan Niesen, "Changing Positions," *Sports Illustrated*, April 16, 2014, http://sportsillustrated.cnn.com/nfl/news/20140416/max-copeland-transformation-2014-nfl-draft/.

43 In a little less . . . lost 50 pounds of fat.: David Morrison, "Missouri Pro Day," *Columbia Daily Tribune*, March 20, 2014, http://columbiatribune.com/blogs/behind_the_stripes/missouri-pro-day-waters-breaks-out-copeland-slims-down/article.

43 When Wilson saw him . . . He doesn't like that.": Niesen, "Changing Positions."

43 Copeland also approached . . . "What a loyal dude.": Morrison, "Missouri Pro Day."

43 at Missouri's Pro Day . . .routes and caught passes: Morrison, "Missouri Pro Day."

43 I'm always changing faces, man. I'm always trying to be unrecognizable.: Morrison, "Missouri Pro Day."

44 Faurot used the newfangled . . . result was a touchdown,: Bill C., "The Greatest Win — Pre-1963 Region (Round One)," *RockMNation.com*, July 30, 2009, http://www.rockmnation.com, 2009/7/30/963737/the-greatest-win-pre-1963-region.

44 Don Faurot made the only . . . offshoot of his old Split T.": Peterson, p. 41.

45 When Vann was born, . . . tattoos relating to God.: David Briggs, "Vann Draws upon Faith, Two Familes for Support," *Columbia Daily Tribune*, Nov. 10, 2010, http://www.columbiatribune.com/sports/mu/vann-draws-upon-faith-two-families-for-support/article.

45 God has played a major role in my life.: Briggs, "Vann Draws Upon Faith."

46 All-American end Conrad . . . around the arena watching.": Marcus Wilkins, "Changing the Culture," *MIZZOU Magazine*, Oct. 25, 2012, https://www.mizzoumag.missouri.edu/2012/10/changing-the-culture/.

46 He had decided on . . . wouldn't have let us vote,": Wilkins, "Changing the Culture."

46 The season was long, . . . a no-name bowl.: Wilkins, "Changing the Culture."

47 the cupcake was laced with . . . could squeak this one out.": Joe Walljasper, "Tigers Got Away with One," *Columbia Daily Tribune*, Sept. 18, 2010, http://www.columbiatribune.com/sports/mu_football/tigers-got-away-with-one/article.

47 In the huddle slot receiver . . . it's time to be great.": Dave Matter, "Last-Minute T.J. Moe Touchdown Saves Tigers from Upset," *Columbia Daily Tribune*, Sept. 18, 2010, http://www.columbiatribune.com/sports/mu_football/last-minute-t-j-moe-touchdown-saves-tigers-from-upset/article.

47   the play that "changed . . . in the first half.": Matter, "Last-Minute T.J. Moe Touch-down."

47   "pure elation replaced embarrassment.": Walljasper, "Tigers Got Away with One."

48   That 1-4 start led head . . . "We really came back,": Broeg, p. 216.

48   Sophomore end Jack Hurley . . . by quarterback Tony Scardino.: Broeg, p. 217.

48   He had not played a . . . the only player left.; Broeg, p. 217.

48   Kansas hit a pass . . . also knocked the ball out.: Broeg, p. 218.

49   a "grinning squirt from . . . a "mighty mite.": Broeg, p. 348.

49   "no more than knee-high to a powder keg.": Tom Lindley, "Missouri Sacks Auburn 34-17," *El Paso Times*, Dec. 29, 1973, reprinted at MIZZOU TIGERS, Dec. 14, 2006, www.mutigers.com/sports/m-footbl/spec-rel/121406aaa.html.

49   Eddie Onofrio, the coach's . . . Moseley a serious look.: Broeg, p. 348.

49   "one of the most exciting players ever to play at MU,": "John Moseley," *MIZZOU TIGERS*, www.mutigers.com/genrel/mosely_john00.html.

49   Gee, Dad, you've just . . . look at John [Moseley].: Broeg, p. 348.

50   "a Ruthian homer": "2012 Season in Review," *2013 Mizzou Baseball Media Guide*, p. 56, grfx.cstv.com/photos/schools/miss/sports/m-basebl/auto_pdf/2012-13/misc_non_event/2013MediaGuideSection3.pdf.

50   He remembered something each . . . T-shirt people again.": *2013 Mizzou Baseball Media Guide*, p. 56.

51   Andy Hill said in 2012 . . . Justin Smith, and Moe.: Dave Matter, "Just as He and His Dad Drew It Up," *Columbia Daily Tribune*, Sept. 1, 2012, http://www.columbiatribune.com/news/2012/sep/01/all-part-of-the-plan/?news.

51   "If you prioritize behind . . . a whole lot of coaxing,": Matter, "Just as He and His Dad Drew It Up."

51   Moe managed to make . . . not be there forever.": Matter, "Just as He and His Dad Drew It Up."

51   [Playing football] is something . . . the rest of your life.: Matter, "Just as He and His Dad Drew It Up."

52   that means the equivalent . . . crank up the washing machines.: Lisa Groshong, "Detail Man," *MIZZOU*, Fall 2007, http://mizzoumagarchives.missouri.edu/2007-fall/features/equip-guy/index.php.

52   Laundry is my life: Groshong, "Detail Man."

53   the goal lines at Rollins Field were 116 yards apart at the time.: Broeg, p. 25.

53   Head coach Frank Patterson asked . . . the Tigers to Dallas anyhow.: Broeg, p. 26.

53   two men came forward with a . . . not at all times strictly decorous.": Broeg, p. 25.

53   The team then crossed "into Mexico . . . had traveled some 6,000 miles.: Broeg, p. 25.

53   An unamused administration fired . . . team manager G.H. English,: Broeg, p. 26.

53   The trip into Mexico . . . had to be heady stuff for the truant Tigers.: Broeg, p. 25.

54   "On both campuses the contempt simmered.": David Briggs, "The Day the Border War Bubbled Over," *Columbia Daily Tribune*, March 5, 2011, http://www.columbiatribune.com/sports/mu_basketball/the-day-the-border-war-bubbled-over/article.

54   Fearing trouble, athletic director . . . without any further fisticuffs.: Briggs, "The Day the Border War Bubbled Over."

54   Turned around just in time for him to smack me right between the eyes.: Briggs, "The Day the Border War Bubbled Over."

55   Daniel dreamed of playing . . . very committed to him.": Dave Matter, "Chasing Texas: Fact and Fiction," *Columbia Daily Tribune*, Oct. 14, 2008, http://www.columbia-tribune.com/sports/chasing-texas-fact-and-fiction/article.

55   When I committed to . . . all other ties.: Dave Matter, "Chasing Texas."

56   Devine relied on the coach's reputation for turning around struggling programs.: Dave Matter, "'He Restored the Roar,'" *Columbia Daily Tribune*, Jan. 29, 2008, http://www.columbiatribune.com/sports/mu_football/he-restored-the-roar/article.

56 a coach much like . . . and a tough defense.: Richardson, p. 201.

56 His first day on . . . physical football at Missouri.: Matter, "'He Restored the Roar.'"

56 Fullback Ron Janes recalled . . . making us tough.": Matter, "'He Restored the Roar.'"

56 practices under Smith . . . though it was midseason.: Richardson, p. 207.

56 "line-it-up and smash mouth," Richardson, p. 210.

56 "the unthinkable" at the time: Matter, "'He Restored the Roar.'"

56 "He restored the roar. He brought the program back to life.": Matter, "'He Restored the Roar.'"

56 [It's] not fancy stuff. You just line up and knock the tar out of the guy over you.: Matter, "'He Restored the Roar.'"

57 Missouri's "defense was getting . . . voices in his headset.": Joe Walljasper, "Tigers Show Knack for Crisis Management," *Columbia Daily Tribune*, Oct. 13, 2013, http://www.columbiadailytribune.com/sports/mu_football/tigers-show-knack-for-crisis-management/article.

57 "validate the Tigers . . . members of the SEC": Matter, "Tigers Show Knack."

57 "When we see adversity, . . . up to each other,": David Morrison, "Missouri Scores Signature Win," *Columbia Daily Tribune*, Oct. 13, 2013, http://www.columbiatribune.com/sports/mu_football/missouri-scores-signature-win-at-georgia-despite-injuries-to-franklin/article.

57 These buys battle . . . a lot of heart.: Morrison, "Missouri Scores Signature Win."

58 "a miraculous win at Ann Arbor": Donoho and O'Brien, "Haas Cleaning," *Mizzou Rah!*, p. 27.

58 "a defensive star with limited ability as a passer": Broeg, p. 245.

58 Haas himself admitted that he wasn't a potent passer.: Donoho and O'Brien, "Haas Cleaning," p. 27.

58 That was the greatest clutch performance I've ever seen.: Broeg, p. 246.

59 "I wouldn't have laughed, . . . what the season would bring.: Steve Walentik, "Ambush of Tigers Tears by Memphis," *Columbia Daily Tribune*, March 26, 2009, http://www.columbiatribune.com/sports/mu_basketball/ambush-of-tigers-tears-by-memphis-into-regioinal-final/article.

59 At the end of every . . . shooter on our team,": Steve Walentik, "Practice Pays Off in Big, Long Way," *Columbia Daily Tribune*, March 27, 2009, http://www.columbiatribune.com/sports/mu_basketball/practice-pays-off-in-big-long-way/article.

59 It was a great shot, . . . a week in practice.: Walentik, "Practice Pays Off."

60 Robinson was only 16 years . . . "had trouble getting players,": Richardson, p. 11.

60 The game was played at the . . . running uphill all season.": Richardson, p. 12.

60 the headline in a Kansas City . . . set up a Tiger touchdown.": Richardson, p. 13.

60 In 1969, Robinson bought a . . . that called him "Van Morrison,": Richardson, p. 13.

60 It was my greatest accomplishment and they misspelled my name.: Richardson, p. 13.

61 With the Nebraska game up next, . . . playing the Chicago Bears,": Richardson, pp. 58-59.

61 Safety Dennis Poppe recalled that . . . he was trying to do.": Richardson, p. 59.

62 "hit the jackpot at football's . . . a quarterback ain't one.": Dave Matter, "Franklin Returns as Tigers Collect First SEC Win," *Columbia Daily Tribune*, Oct. 27, 2012, http://www.columbiatribune.com/sports/mu_football/franklin-returns-as-tigers-collect-first-sec-win/article.

62 For the first time since . . . to start his backup.: Matter, "Franklin Returns."

62 For the first time in his . . . a run-at-all-costs approach,: Matter, "Franklin Returns."

62 the fewest for the . . . a win over Baylor in 2005: Matter, "Franklin Returns."

62 You do what's the best call for your team.: Matter, "Franklin Returns."

63 She verbally committed to . . . to be at the University of Missouri.": Jenna Sampson, "The Return of a Dream," *Sharing the Victory*, April

2011, http://archives.fca.org/vsItemDisplay.1sp?method=display&objectid=042B86 AD.

63   I can look back and see that God had a reason for bringing me here.: Sampson, "The Return of a Dream."

64   Grant Ressel attempted only . . . him to go do that.'": Joe Walljasper, "From Barely Noticed Walk-On to One of Nation's Top Kickers," *Columbia Daily Tribune*, Nov. 27, 2010, http://www.columbiatribune.com/sports/mu_football/from-barely-noticed-walk-on-to-one-of-nation-s/article.

64   Don't know what's going on. They don't answer your calls or anything.: Walljasper, "From Barely Noticed Walk-On."

65   "purg[ed] a 15-game . . . the nation's football cathedrals.": Gregorian, "Seeing Red," *Mizzou-RAH!*, p. 73.

65   After the game, Missouri . . . schemes to foil Mizzou.": Gregorian, "Seeing Red," *Mizzou-RAH!*, p. 75.

65   "They wanted to shut us . . . minute of the game (starting).": Gregorian, "Seeing Red," *Mizzou-RAH!*, p. 77.

65   The Tigers never had to punt.: Gregorian, "Seeing Red," *Mizzou-RAH!*, p. 75.

65   We're going to have . . . that's not reality.: Gregorian, "Seeing Red," *Mizzou-RAH!*, p. 75.

66   In 1891 a field was set aside . . . students built wooden bleachers.: "Mizzourah! Football at MU: The Early Years," *Archives of the University of Missouri*, muarchives.missouri.edu/football2.html.

66   According to Art Nebel, a student . . . down there under the gridiron,": Broeg, p. 86.

66   Three days before the game, . . . the state highway department.: Broeg, p. 86.

66   The steady downpour meant the . . . field into one big mudhole.: Broeg, p. 88.

66   The game was scoreless — a mudpie tie.: Broeg, p. 88.

67   "I thought the game was pretty much over,": David Briggs, "MU Women Stage Stunning Rally, Top Texas in OT" *Columbia Daily Tribune*, Jan. 9, 2011, http://www.columbiatribune.com/sports/mu_basketball/mu-women-stage-stunning-rally-top-texas-in-ot/article.

67   Missouri had used only . . . in her 26-year coaching career.: Briggs, "MU Women Stage Stunning Rally."

67   "They kept playing and we didn't,": Briggs, "MU Women Stage Stunning Rally."

67   I didn't see any quit in our kids.: Briggs, "MU Women Stage Stunning Rally."

68   It was described as "virtually flawless.": "Beau Brinkley," MIZZOU TIGERS, http://www.mutigers.com/sports/m-footbl/brinkley_beau00.html.

68   From the first, though, . . . all the long snapping chores.: Dave Matter, "Brinkley's Rise to First String Is a Snap," *Columbia Daily Tribune*, Sept. 22, 2009, http://www.columbiatribune.com/sports/mu_football/brinkley-s-rise-to-first-string-is-a-snap/article.

68   Who would have thought I'd be out here where I am right now?: Matter, "Brinkley's Rise to First String Is a Snap."

69   With a mother who was . . . a gallon of mouthwash.": Broeg, p. 237.

69   If you're looking for a . . . would call a 'fussbudget.': Broeg, p. 237.

70   He "emerged as one of college football's brightest stars.": Donoho and O'Brien, "Uncle Don and Pitchin' Paul," *MizzouRah!*, p. 11.

70   "with all the nonchalance of a coed powdering her nose at the junior prom.": Donoho and O'Brien, "Uncle Don and Pitchin' Paul," *MizzouRah!* p. 11.

70   Christman personally outgained . . . country stole the show.": Donoho and O'Brien, "Uncle Don and Pitchin' Paul," *Mizzourah!* p. 12.

70   more than 2,000 UM . . . train rolled into Columbia.: Donoho and O'Brien, "Uncle Don and Pitchin' Paul," *Mizzourah!* p. 12.

70   One game, more than any other, established Mizzou's national prominence.: Donoho and O'Brien, "Uncle Don and Pitchin' Paul," *Mizzourah!* p. 11.

71   The $100 the team netted from . . . willingly paid a $1 initiation fee.: Broeg, p. 21.

71   With interest in the school's . . . cost was $3 per week per player.: Broeg, p. 22.

71   By 1895, admission prices to . . . Kansas game at Kansas City.: Broeg, p. 23.

71   With athletic funds sagging in . . . the team's practice sessions.: Broeg, p. 24.

71   The Tigers cleared $5,000 alone from the Kansas game.: Broeg, p. 29.

71   Expenses in 1903 totaled about . . . expenses were another $1,800.: Broeg, p. 32.

71   by 1904, John F. McLean was . . . whopping sum of $2,000 to coach.: Broeg, p. 32.

71   As usual, in 1896, there . . . Pop Bliss -- for two months.: Broeg, p. 24.

72   was passed over both times . . . board of curators came next.: Steve Walentik, "Anderson Takes the Long Way Home," *Columbia Daily Tribune*, April 29, 2014, http://www.columbiatribune.com/sports/mu_basketball/anderson-takes-the-long-way-home-to-mu/article.

72   I wouldn't have hired me either in 1999. I wasn't ready.: Walentik, "Anderson Takes the Long Way Home."

73   "everyone thought [his] visor had cut off circulation to his brain.": Joe Walljasper, "Best-Laid Plans," *Columbia Daily Tribune*, Nov. 29, 2009, http://www.columbiatribune.com/sports/mu_football/best-laid-plans-even-if-they-are-sketchy-don-t/article.

73   a defense "that had been . . . to join the unemployment line.: Walljasper, "Best-Laid Plans."

73   "the kicker with the face of Opie Taylor and the nerves of a burglar,": Walljasper, "Best-Laid Plans."

73   I thought everybody thought . . . I guess it was KU fans.: Walljasper, "Best-Laid Plans."

74   cut to his left behind . . . Moseley's "pulsating gallop": Lindley, "Missouri Sacks Auburn 34-17."

74   It was definitely the key play of the game.: Lindley, "Missouri Sacks Auburn 34-17."

75   Tiger football players were not . . . worried about playing Texas.: Dave Matter, "Following Pinkel's Lead, Tigers Mum on SEC," *Columbia Daily Tribune*, Nov. 8, 2011, http://www.columbiatribune.com/sports/mu_football/following-pinkel-s-lead-tigers-mum-on-sec/article.

75   "a game of SEC football." . . . in the SEC slugfests.": Dave Matter, "Pinkel, Tigers Finally Take Down Longhorns," *Columbia Daily Tribune*, Nov. 12, 2011, http://www.columbiatribune.com/sports/mu_football/pinkel-tigers-finally-take-down-longhorns/article.

75   "They wanted to run the ball. We stopped the run,": Matter, "Pinkel, Tigers Finally Take Down Longhorns."

75   I really do not care . . . getting them a win Saturday": Matter, "Following Pinkel's Lead, Tigers Mum on SEC."

76   After the 1908 football season, . . . you want to beat Kansas,": Broeg, p. 37.

76   "neither innovator nor taskmaster," . . . "He was a great psychologist,": Broeg, p. 38.

76   He installed what he called . . . won't be beat, can't be beat.": Broeg, p. 40.

76   a much bigger paycheck took him back to Princeton: Broeg, p. 42.

76   He was wonderful in talking to the team.: Broeg, p. 38.

77   "Our team bus driver was . . . an overmatched Colorado team.: Marcus Wilkins, "The Boys of Summer," *MIZZOU Magazine*, Feb. 17, 2014, mizzoumag.missouri.edu/2014/02/the-boys-of-summer.

77   My fear was that . . . give myself away.: Wilkins, "The Boys of Summer."

78   "Many times the first . . . why I did this,": Vahe Gregorian, "It Takes Everybody," *Mizzou-RAH!* (St. Louis: St. Louis Post-Dispatch Books, 2012), p. 26.

78	"were on the verge of a potentially season-defining setback, " Gregorian, "It Takes Everybody," p. 27.
78	I mean, he did what you can't do.: Gregorian, "It Takes Everybody," p. 27.
79	the pillows of the place where they stayed said "Roll Tide!": Richardson, p. 89.
79	"Man, we are in Bama . . . gets a standing ovation.: Richardson, p. 89.
79	I don't think they thought of Missouri as a worthy opponent.": Richardson, p. 88.
79	Roger Wehrli, who honeymooned at the Gator Bowl,: Donoho and O'Brien, "Horse-whipped!" *Mizzourah!* p. 52.
79	Bear Bryant was the king down there.: Richardson, p. 88.
80	a record crowd of nearly . . . big ball game, that's for sure,": Peterson, p. 6.
80	"considered by many the . . . Don Faurot ever coached,": Peterson, p. 6.
80	"remembered as one of the best in school history.": Peterson, p. 7.
80	Nobody expected us to win, but we got the upset.: Peterson, p. 6.
81	Marching music began at . . . furnished their own music,: Nancy Moen and Ryan Gavin, "Big, Brassy Marching Mizzou," *Mizzou Wire*, Sept. 3, 2010, http://mizzou wire.missouri.edu/stories/2010/marching-mizzou/index.php.
81	The band played classical . . . modernism known as jazz.": Moen and Gavin.
81	women joined the ranks in . . . and one to beat it.: Moen and Gavin.
81	The more noise, the more spirit.: Moen and Gavin.
82	As Corby Jones prepared to . . . and kiss him on the head.: Tim Layden, "Heavy Heart," *Sports Illustrated*, Sept. 21, 1998, http://sportsillustrated.cnn.com/vault/article/magazine/MAG1014051/index.htm.
82	"He controlled everything . . . what seemed like hours.": Layden, "Heavy Heart."
82	"To have Corby with him . . . "He was ecstatic.": Layden, "Heavy Heart."
82	Over the years he gave . . . them better than ever.: Layden, "Heavy Heart."
83	"His statistics were mediocre,": Dave Matter, "Low-Key Johnson Made Big Impact in NFL," *Columbia Daily Tribune*, Jan. 22. 2010, http://www.columbiatribune.com/sports/mu_football/low-key-johnson-made-big-impact-in-nfl/article.
83	"defensive specialist who ran much better than he threw.": Broeg, p. 265.
83	John Kadlec recalled that . . . you're going to get hit.": Matter, "Low-Key Johnson."
83	a "defensive mastermind.": Matter, "Low-Key Johnson."
83	"complicated schemes that pressured . . . "a pioneering and brilliant strategist.": Richard Goldstein, "Jim Johnson, Innovative Defensive Assistant in the N.F.L., Dies at 68," *The New York Times*, July 29, 2009, http://www.nytimes.com/2009/07/30/sports/football/30johnson.html?_r=0.
83	He wasn't a star, . . . a lot out of what he had.: Matter, "Low-Key Johnson."
84	Henry scheduled both intersectional . . . some attention to Columbia.: Broeg, p. 74.
84	"a trim, spectacled Texan . . . better known as a track coach;: Broeg, p. 68.
84	They rushed for 327 yards . . . all intercepted passes.: Broeg, p. 93.
84	After the touchdown, Flamank . . . limped out of the game.: Broeg, p. 95.
84	Funny thing about it, but I didn't really throw that many passes.: Broeg, p. 93.
85	When Hainey was 12, . . . couldn't promise her anything.: David Briggs, "Just Give Her the Ball," *Columbia Daily Tribune*, May 1, 2010, http://www.columbiatribune.com/sports/mu/just-give-her-the-ball/article.
85	That's when Christopher, a . . . "Everything is working.": David Briggs, "MU Softball in Title Game," *Columbia Daily Tribune*, May 16, 2010, http://www.columbia tribune.com/sports/mu/mu-softball-in-title-game/article.
85	We needed revenge. . . . getting them back.: Briggs, "MU Softball in Title Game."
86	During the 22-21 road . . . at the next home game.: Donoho and O'Brien, "M-I-Z! Z-O-U!" *MizzouRah!*, p. 95.
86	the idea went "over a bit . . . the crowd to provide instructions: Donoho and O'Brien, "M-I-Z! Z-O-U!" *MizzouRah!*, p. 96.

86   "We all knew it was going to work,": Donoho and O'Brien, "M-I-Z! Z-O-U!" *MizzouRah!*, p. 97.

86   A bunch of creative . . . generations to come.: Donoho and O'Brien, "M-I-Z! Z-O-U!" *MizzouRah!*, p. 98.

87   "He's a special guy in so many ways,": Dave Matter, "Grandpa Knew Best All Along," *Columbia Daily Tribune*, Nov. 5, 2008, http://www.columbiatribune.com/ sports/grandpa-knew-best-all-along/article.

87   After MU's 2004 spring . . . he was exactly right.": Matter, "Grandpa Knew Best."

87   Saunders' grandfather died . . . had known all along.: Matter, "Grandpa Knew Best."

87   "a purely selfish . . . misfortune or frustration": Bruce T. Dahlberg, "Anger," *The Interpreter's Dictionary of the Bible* (Nashville: Abingdon Press, 1962), Vol. 1, p. 136.

87   [Tommy Saunders'] grandfather did not really care for me.: Matter, "Grandpa Knew Best."

88   who had seen only one . . . stood tall physically and morally,: Broeg, p. 62.

88   "a raucous character who . . . coach's immediate resignation.: Broeg, p. 65.

89   A "tremendously talented Kansas team": Broeg, p. 255.

90   "grab-bag of 4-Fs and baby faces": Atchison, p. 88.

90   what they did "seemed like utter triumph.": Atchison, p. 91.

90   students "too young to . . . or deferred from service.": Atchison, p. 88.

90   not a single starter of . . . a boy among men on most nights.": Atchison, p. 88.

90   Because navy regulations restricted . . . away from the base,: Atchison, p. 91.

90   Edwards's innocents were baptized by fire.: Atchison, p. 88.

91   "didn't seem to belong with . . . Big 12 ways wouldn't work": Joe Walljasper, " Tigers Prove They Have SEC Substance," *Columbia Daily Tribune*, Nov. 24, 2013, http://www.columbiatribune.com/sports/tigersextra/tigers-prove-they-have-sec-substance/article.

91   Thirteen straight times . . . the SEC's championship game.: Walljasper, "Tigers Prove They Have SEC Substance."

91   What they are is . . . games in the trenches.: Walljasper, "Tigers Prove They Have SEC Substance."

92   football games were what he called "a glorious workout.": Cory Walton, "Mizzou Welcomes No. 27 Home," *MIZZOU TIGERS,* Sept. 13, 2003, http://www.mutigers. com/sports/m-footbl/spec-rel/091403aab.html.

92   "Game day was easy for . . . biggest or the strongest,": Walton, "Mizzou Welcomes No. 27 Home."

92   I made my legacy off the football field in preparation for game day.: Walton, "Mizzou Welcomes No. 27 Home."

93   Missouri teams never panic and never will.": Broeg, p. 310.

93   Big Eight commissioner Wayne Duke . . . from five bowls looking on,.: Broeg, p. 310.

93   in the space of seven seconds . . . the first play after the kick.: Broeg, p. 310.

94   "I was kind of going . . . time for him to go.: Dave Matter, "Maclin Bids Tearful Farewell to Tigers," *Columbia Daily Tribune*, Jan. 8, 2009, http://www.columbia tribune.com/sports/maclin-bids-tearful-farewell-to-tigers/article.

94   I'm leaving a family. All those guys are like father figures to me.: Matter, "Maclin Bids Tearful Farewell to Tigers."

WORKS CITED

"2012 Season in Review." *2013 Mizzou Baseball Media Guide.* 56. grfx.cstv.com/photos/schools/miss/sports/m-basebl/auto_pdf/misc_non_event/2013MediaGuideSection3.pdf.

Atchison, Michael. *True Sons: A Century of Missouri Tigers Basketball.* Virginia Beach, Va.: The Donning Company Publishers, 2006.

"Beau Brinkley." *MIZZOU TIGERS.* http://www.mutigers.com/sports/m-footbl/brinkley_beau00.html.

Bettinger, Jim & Julie S. *The Book of Bowden.* Nashville: TowleHouse Publishing, 2001.

Briggs, David. "Just Give Her the Ball." *Columbia Daily Tribune.* 1 May 2010. http://www.columbiatribune.com/sports/mu/just-give-her-the-ball/article.

-----. "MU Softball in Title Game." *Columbia Daily Tribune.* 16 May 2010. http://www.columbiatribune.com/sports/mu/mu-softball-in-title-game/article.

-----. "MU Women Stage Stunning Rally." *Columbia Daily Tribune.* 9 Jan. 2011. http://www.columbiatribune.com/sports/mu_basketball/mu-women-stage-stunning-rally-top-texas-in-ot/article.

-----. "The Day the Border War Bubbled Over." *Columbia Daily Tribune.* 5 March 2011. http://www.columbiatribune.com/sports/mu_basketball/the-day-the-border-war-bubbled-over/article.

-----. "They've Come a Long Way, Baby." *Columbia Daily Tribune.* 26 Oct. 2009. http://www.columbiatribune.com/sports/mu/they-ve-come-a-long-way-baby/article.

-----. "Vann Draws upon Faith, Two Families for Support." *Columbia Daily Tribune.* 10 Nov. 2010. http://www.columbiatribune.com/sports/mu/vann-draws-upon-faith-two-families-for-support/article.

Broeg, Bob. *Ol' Mizzou: A Story of Missouri Football.* Huntsville, AL: The Strode Publishers, 1974.

C, Bill. "The Greatest Win – Pre-1963 Region (Round One)." *RockMNation.com.* 30 July 2009. http://www.rockmnation.com/2009/7/30/963737/the-greatest-win-pre-1963-region.

Carter, Bo. "From the Diving Board to 90,000-Seat Football Stadiums, Missouri Kicker Jeff Wolfert Still Making Waves." *National Football Foundation.* 9 Nov. 2008. http://www.footballfoundation.org/tabid/567/article/51840.

Coats, Bill. "At Last! MU Snaps Quarter-Century Losing Streak vs. Nebraska." *Mizzou-RAH! Celebrating MU's Football Revival, and the Tigers' Leap to the SEC.* St. Louis: St. Louis Post-Dispatch Books, 2012. 68-71.

"College Days: Roger Wehrli." *profootballhof.com.* http://www.profootballhof.com/story/2013/12/5/college-days-roger-wehrli/.

Dahlberg, Bruce T. "Anger." *The Interpreter's Dictionary of the Bible.* Nashville: Abingdon Press, 1962. Vol. 1. 135-37.

Dellenger, Ross. "Eye Climbing Closer to MU, NCAA Marks." *Columbia Daily Tribune.* 10 Feb. 2013. http://www.columbiatribune.com/sports/mu_basketball/eye-climbing-closer-to-mu-ncaa-marks/article.

-----. "Josey Says He Has 'Good Chance' to Play in 2012." *Columbia Daily Tribune.* 3 Aug. 2012. http://www.columbiatribune.com/sports/mu_football/josey-says-he-has-good-chance-to-play-in/article.

Donoho, Todd and Dan O'Brien. "Al's Well That Ends Well." *Mizzourah! Memorable Moments in Missouri Tiger Football History.* Virginia Beach, Va.: The Donning Company Publishers, 2004. 67-69.

-----. "Brown Out." *Mizzourah! Memorable Moments in Missouri Tiger Football History.* Virginia Beach, Va.: The Donning Company Publishers, 2004. 55-56.

-----. "Haas Cleaning." *Mizzourah! Memorable Moments in Missouri Tiger Football History.* Virginia Beach, Va.: The Donning Company Publishers, 2004. 27-29.

-----. "Horsewhipped!" *Mizzourah! Memorable Moments in Missouri Tiger Football History.* Virginia Beach, Va.: The Donning Company Publishers, 2004. 51-53.

-----. "M-I-Z! Z-O-U!" *MizzouRah!. Memorable Moments in Missouri Tiger Football History.* Virginia Beach, Va.: The Donning Company Publishers, 2004. 95-98.

-----. "Trojans Fed to Tigers at Coliseum." *Mizzourah! Memorable Moments in Missouri Tiger Football History.* Virginia Beach, Va.: The Donning Company Publishers, 2004. 83-84.

-----. "Uncle Don and Pitchin' Paul." *Mizzourah! Memorable Moments in Missouri Tiger Football History*. Virginia Beach, Va.: The Donning Company Publishers, 2004. 11-13.

Fallstrom, R.B. "Mr. Perfect Jeff Wolfert Missouri Tigers' Hidden Asset." *Lubbock Avalanche-Journal*. 30 Nov. 2007. lubbockonline.com/stories/113007/col_113007012.shtml.

Forde, Pat. "Molded by His Mentor, Gary Pinkel Has Pushed Missouri into Prime Time in SEC." *Yahoo Sports*. 29 Nov. 2013. http://sports.yahoo.com/ncaaf--molded-by-his-mentor--gary-pinkel-has-pushed-missouri-into-prime-time-in-sec-154705507.html.

"Game Notes: Missouri 51, Tennessee 48 (4OT)." *Columbia Daily Tribune*. 11 Nov. 2012. http://www.missouritribune.com/sports/mu_football/game-notes-missouri-tennessee-ot/article.

Gavin, Ryan. "Gymnast's Long Journey." *Mizzou Wire*. 5 May 2010. http://mizzouwire.missouri.edu/stories/2010/sarah-shire/index.php.

-----. "Mark of a Champion." *Mizzou Wire*. 28 April 2009. http://mizzouwire.missouri.edu/stories/2009/mark-champion/index.php.

Goldstein, Richard. "Jim Johnson, Innovative Defensive Assistant in the N.F.L., Dies at 68." *The New York Times*. 29 July 2009. http://www.nytimes.com/2009/07/30/sports/football/30johnson.html?_r=0.

Gregorian, Vahe. "It Takes Everybody, Not Just Gary Pinkel." *Mizzou-RAH! Celebrating MU's Football Revival, and the Tigers' Leap to the SEC*. St. Louis: St. Louis Post-Dispatch Books, 2012. 24-29.

-----. "One Lost, Now Found: William Moore." *Mizzou-RAH! Celebrating MU's Football Revival, and the Tigers' Leap to the SEC*. St. Louis: St. Louis Post-Dispatch Books, 2012. 105-111.

-----. "Mizzou's Leading Man: Brad Smith." *Mizzou-RAH! Celebrating MU's Football Revival, and the Tigers' Leap to the SEC*. St. Louis: St. Louis Post-Dispatch Books, 2012. 84-93.

-----. "Seeing Red: Tigers Settle Old Scores in Lincoln." *Mizzou-RAH! Celebrating MU's Football Revival, and the Tigers' Leap to the SEC*. St. Louis: St. Louis Post-Dispatch Books, 2012. 73-77.

Groshong, Lisa. "Detail Man." *MIZZOU*. Fall 2007. http://mizzoumagarchives.missouri.edu/2007-fall/feagures/equip-guy/index.php.

"John Kadlec Retires from MU Football Broadcast Booth." *MIZZOU TIGERS*. 31 Jan. 2011. http://www.mutigers.com/sports/m-footbl/spec-rel/013111aaa.html.

"John Moseley," *MIZZOU TIGERS*. www.mutigers.com/genrel/moseley_john00.html.

Keller, Rudi. "Anniversary Approaches for Origin of MU Tiger Nickname." *Columbia Daily Tribune*. 6 July 2014. http://www.columbiatribune.com/news/civil_war/anniversary-approaches-for-irigin-of-mu-tiger-nickname/article.

"Kreklow, Henning Named Volleyball Magazine All-Americans." *MIZZOU TIGERS*. 20 Jan. 20, 2014. http://www.mutigers.com/sports-w-volley/spec-rel/012014aaa.html.

Layden, Tim. "Heavy Heart." *Sports Illustrated*. 21 Sept. 1998. http://sportsillustrated.cnn.com/vault/article/magazine/MAG1014051/index.htm.

Lindley, Tom. "Missouri Sacks Auburn 34-17 on Game-Breaking Runback." *El Paso Times*. 29 Dec. 1973. Reprinted at *MIZZOU TIGERS*. 14 Dec. 2006. http://www.mutigers.com/sports/m-footbl/spec-rel/121406aaa.html.

Makowski, Marek. "For Molly Kreklow, Home and the Road." *The Maneater*. 10 Sept. 2013. http://www.themaneaster.com/stories/2013/9/10/molly-kreklow-home-and-road/.

Matter, Dave. "All Now Bright for Fisher After Devastating Injury." *Columbia Daily Tribune*. 18 Dec. 2011. http://www.columbiatribune.com/sports/mu_football/all-now-bright-for-fisher-after-devastating-injury/article.

-----. "Brinkley's Rise to First String Is a Snap." *Columbia Daily Tribune*. 22 Sept. 2009. http://www.columbiatribune.com/sports/mu_football/brinkley-s-rise-to-first-string-is-a-snap/article.

-----. "Chasing Texas: Fact and Fiction." *Columbia Daily Tribune*. 14 Oct. 2008. http://www.columbia-tribune.com/sports/chasing-texas-fact-and-fiction/article.

-----. "Following Pinkel's Lead, Tigers Mum on SEC.": *Columbia Daily Tribune*. 8 Nov. 2011. http://www.columbiatribune.com/sports/mu_football/following-pinkel-s-lead-tigers-mum-on-sec/article.

-----. "Franklin Returns as Tigers Collect First SEC Win." *Columbia Daily Tribune*. 27 Oct. 2012. http://www.columbiatribune.com/sports/mu_football/franklin-returns-as-tigers-collect-first-sec-win/article.

-----. "Grandpa Knew Best All Along." *Columbia Daily Tribune*. http://www.columbiatribune.com/sports/grandpa-knew-best-all-along/article.

-----. "Happy at Home." *Columbia Daily Tribune*. 19 April 2008. http://www.columbiatribune.com/sports/happy-at-home/article.

-----. "'He Restored the Roar.'" *Columbia Daily Tribune*. 29 Jan. 2008. http://www.columbiatribune.com./sports/mu_football/he-restored-the-roar/article.

-----. "Just as He and His Dad Drew It Up, Moe Has Worked His Way into MU Lore." *Columbia Daily Tribune*. 1 Sept. 2012. http://www.columbiatribune.com/news/2012/sept/01/all-part-of-the-plan/?news.

-----. "Knee Injury Shapes Josey's Decision to Enter Draft." *St. Louis Post-Dispatch*. 8 Jan. 2014. http://www.stltoday.com/sports/college/mizzou/knee-injury-shapes-josey-s-decision-to-enter-draft/article.

-----. "Last-Minute T.J. Moe Touchdown Saves Tigers from Upset." *Columbia Daily Tribune*. 18 Sept. 2010. http://www.columbiatribune.com/sports/mu_football/last-minute-t-j-moe-touchdown-saves-tigers-from-upset/article.

-----. "Low-Key Johnson Made Big Impact in NFL." *Columbia Daily Tribune*. 22 Jan. 2010. http://www.columbiatribune.com/sports/mu_football/low-key-johnson-made-big-impact-in-nfl/article.

-----. "Maclin Bids Tearful Farewell to Tigers." *Columbia Daily Tribune*. 8 Jan. 2009. http://www.columbiatribune.com/sports/maclin-bids-tearful-farewell-to-tigers/article.

-----. "Pinkel, Tigers Finally Take Down Longhorns." *Columbia Daily Tribune*. 12 Nov. 2011. http://www.columbiatribune.com/sports/mu_football/pinkel-tigers-finally-take-down-longhorns/article.

-----. "The Old Man and the Knee." *Columbia Daily Tribune*. 7 March 2012. http://www.columbiatribune.com/sports/mu_football/the-old-man-and-the-knee/article.

"Max Copeland." *MIZZOU TIGERS*. http://www.mutigers.com/sports/m-footbl/mtt/max_copeland_465234.html.

"Missouri Civil War Sesquicentennial: William T. 'Bloody Bill' Anderson." http://civilwar150.com/history/figure/210.

"Mizzourah! Football at MU: The Early Years." *Archives of the University of Missouri*. muarchives.missouri.edu/football2.html.

"Mizzou's Greatest, #82: 1964 Baseball and Its Incredible Pitching Staff." *Rock M Nation*. 24 May 2013. http://www.rockmnation.com/2013/5/24/4362100/1964-missouri-baseball-hi-simmons.

Moen, Nancy and Ryan Gavin. "Big, Brassy Marching Mizzou." *Mizzou Wire*. 3 Sept. 2010. http://mizzouwire.missouri.edu/stories/2010/marching-mizzou/index.php.

Morrison, David. "Josey TD Sends Missouri to SEC East Title in Win over Texas A&M." *Columbia Daily Tribune*. 30 Nov. 2013. http://www.columbiatribunecom/sports/jose-td-sends-missouri-to-sec-east-title-in-win/article.

-----. "Missouri Pro Day: Waters Breaks Out, Copeland Slims Down." *Columbia Daily Tribune*. 20 March 2014. http://www.columbiatribune.com/blogs/behind_the_stripes/missouri-pro-day-waters-breaks-out-copeland-slims-down/article.

-----. "Missouri Scores Signature Win at Georgia, Despite Injuries to Franklin, Gaines." *Columbia Daily Tribune*. 13 Oct. 2013. http://www.columbiatribune.com/sports/mu_football/missouri-scores-signature-win-at-georgia-despite-injuries-to-franklin/article.

Niesen, Joan. "Changing Positions Just Latest Reinvention for Mizzou's Max Copeland." *Sports Illustrated*. 16 April 2014. http://sportsillustrated.cnn.com/nfl/news/20140416/max-copeland-transformation-2014-nfl-draft/.

"No. 5 Missouri Wins SEC East." *Sports Illustrated*. 30 Nov. 2013. http://sportsillustrated.cnn.com/football/ncaa/gameflash/2013/11/30/52600/index.html.

Palmer, Tod. "Senior Molly Kreklow Helps MU Volleyball to Brink of First SEC Title." *The Kansas City Star*. 21 Nov. 2013. http://www.kansascity.com/2013/11/21/4640232/senior-molly-kreklow-helps-mu.html.

Peterson, Brian C. *Stadium Stories: Missouri Tigers*. Guilford, Conn.: The Globe Pequot Press, 2005.

Richardson, Steve. *"Then Pinkel Said to Smith. . .": The Best Missouri Tigers Stories Ever Told*. Chicago: Triumph Books, 2008.

Sampson, Jenna. "The Return of a Dream." *Sharing the Victory*. April 2011. http://archives.fca.org/vsItemDisplay.1sp?method=display&objectid=042B86AD.

Schur, Matthew. "Former MU Quarterback Chase Patton Is Chasing New Dream." *VOX Magazine*. 1 Sept. 2011. archive.voxmagazine.com/stories/2011/09/01/former-mu-quarterback-chase-patton-is-chasing-new-dream/.

Timmerman, Tom. "Breakthrough: Tigers Score Rousing Victory over Longtime Bully Oklahoma." *Mizzou-RAH! Celebrating MU's Football Revival, and the Tigers' Leap to the SEC*. St. Louis: St. Louis Post-Dispatch Books, 2012. 53-57.

Walentik, Steve. "Ambush of Tigers Tears by Memphis into Regional Final." *Columbia Daily Tribune*. 26 March 2009. http://www.columbiatribune.com/sports/mu_basketball/ambush-of-tigers-tears-by-memphis-into-regional-final/article.

-----. "Anderson Takes the Long Way Home to MU." *Columbia Daily Tribune*. 29 April 2014. http://www.columbiatribune.com/sports/mu_basketball/anderson-takes-the-long-way-home-to-mu/article.

-----. "Practice Pays Off in Big, Long Way." *Columbia Daily Tribune*. 27 March 2009. http://www.columbiatribune.com/sports/mu_basketball/practice-pays-off-in-big-long-way/article.

Walljasper, Joe. "Best-Laid Plans, Even if They Are Sketchy, Don't Go Astray." *Columbia Daily Tribune*. 29 Nov. 2009. http://www.columbiatribune.com/sports/mu_football/best-laid-plans-even-if-they-are-sketchy-don-t-/article.

-----. "From Barely Noticed Walk-On to One of Nation's Top Kickers, Ressel Consistent." *Columbia Daily Tribune*. 27 Nov. 2010. http://www.columbiatribune.com/sports/mu_football/from-barely-noticed-walk-on-to-one-of- nation-s/article.

-----. "Mauk Aces Final Exam as Missouri Starter." *Columbia Daily Tribune*. 10 Nov. 2013. http://www.columbiatribune.com/sports/mu_football/mauk-aces-final-exam-as-missouri-starter/article.

-----. "Mr. Big Shot Strikes Again for Missouri." *Columbia Daily Tribune*. 10 Feb. 2009. http://www.columbiatribune.com/sports/mu_basketball/mr-big-shot-strikes-again-for-missouri/article.

-----. "Plenty of Credit to Go Around." *Columbia Daily Tribune*. 26 Oct. 2009. http://www.columbia-tribune.com/sports/mu/plenty-of-credit-to-go-around/article.

-----. "Tigers Got Away with One." *Columbia Daily Tribune*. 18 Sept. 2010. http://www.columbia tribune.com/sports/mu_football/tigers-got-away-with-one/article.

-----. "Tigers Prove They Have SEC Substance." *Columbia Daily Tribune*. 24 Nov. 2013. http://www.columbiatribune.com/sports/tigersextra/tigers-prove-they-have-sec-substance/article.

-----. "Tigers Show Knack for Crisis Management." *Columbia Daily Tribune*. 13 Oct. 2013. http://www.columbiatribune.com/sports/mu_football/tigers-show-knack-for-crisis-management/article.

Walton, Cory. "Mizzou Welcomes No. 27 Home." *MIZZOU TIGERS*. 13 Sept. 2003. http://www.mutigers.com/sports/m-footbl/spec-rel/091403aab.html.

Watson, Graham. "In Cotton Bowl, Tigers Run Hog Wild." *Mizzou-RAH! Celebrating MU's Football Revival, and the Tigers' Leap to the SEC*. St. Louis: St. Louis Post-Dispatch Books, 2012. 62-67.

Wilkins, Marcus. "Changing the Culture." *MIZZOU Magazine*. 25 Oct. 2012. https://mizzoumag.missouri.edu/2012/10/changing-the-culture/.

-----. "Flamethrower: Senior Pitcher Chelsea Thomas Hurls." *MIZZOU Magazine*. 13 Feb. 2013. https://mizzoumag.missouri.edu/2013/02/flamethrower/.

-----. "The Boys of Summer." *MIZZOU Magazine*. 17 Feb. 2014. https://mizzoumag.missouri.edu/2014/02/the-boys-of-summer/.

"Wolfert's 34-Yard Field Goal Helps Missouri Escape with Win." *ESPN*. 1 Nov. 2008. scores.espn.go.com/net/recap?gameId=283060239.

NAME INDEX
(LAST NAME, DEVOTION DAY NUMBER)

Alden, Mike 72, 75
Anderson, Kim 72
Anderson, Mike 29
Anderson, William T. 21
Andrighetto, Kristin 15
Aniston, Jennifer 39
Askren, Ben 41
Atchison, Michael 20, 90
Atkins, Mark 36
Barnes Don 52
Bauman, Bob 77
Beal, Norm 89
Bellino, Joe 89
Bellman, Dottie 86
Blees, Billy 31
Bliss, Pop 71
Blitz, Bryan 15
Boehm, Evan 91
Bond, Art 26
Booker, Melvin 36
Bowden, Bobby 8
Braznell, Dick 80
Brewer, Chester 31
Brinkley, Beau 68
Brinkman, Loyd 80
Britt, Justin 12, 39, 91
Broeg, Bob 1, 9, 19, 30, 53, 66, 69, 71
Brown, Blake 50
Brown, Curtis 34
Brown, Henry 40
Brown, Miller 84
Brown RaeShara 67
Browning, Arthur 20
Browning, Pidge 20
Broyles, Frank 17, 27
Bryant, Bear 79
Bunker, Herb 20, 33, 60, 88
Bushyhead, Jess 86
Byars, Bob 84
Bybee, Ray 74
Caldwell, Charley 76
Callahan, Bill 30
Carras, Nick 48
Carroll, Mike 40
Carter, Win 80
Castiglione, Joe 42
Castle, Bob 48
Chaney, Lon 9
Cherry, John 5
Christman, Paul 19, 44, 70
Christopher, Brock 29, 65
Christopher, Megan 85
Clark, Bert 84
Clemensen, Stub 37

Coffey, Sean 78
Coffman, Chase 29
Collins, Michelle 15
Collins, Paul 33
Cook, Ed 77
Cook, Greg 79
Cooper, Clay 22
Copeland, Max 43, 57, 91
Coulter, Brian 73
Cousin Itt 39
Cox, Buddy 77
Crawford, Carl 46
Crossett, Adam 78
Crowder, Enoch H. 81
Crudup, Jevon 36
D'Amato, Cus 48
Daniel, Chase 6, 16, 18, 23, 29, 55, 65, 78
Daniel, Vickie 55
Daugherty, Duffy 17
Deaton, Brady 75
Dellastatious, Bill 33
Dellenger, Ross 11
Denmon, Marcus 59
Devine, Dan 4, 12, 17, 22, 30, 44, 46, 56, 58, 61, 69, 79, 80, 83, 89, 93
Diemund, Earl 84
Dittamore, Tasha 15
Doane, Dave 37
Donoho, Todd 34, 70, 86
Dorrance, Anson 15
Drass, Rob 25
Drumm, Enoch 84
Duke, Wayne 93
Durocher, Leo 26
Earleywine, Ehren 32, 85
Eberflus, Matt 35
Edwards, George 90
Edwards, Kip 75
Ekern, Bill 33
Ellis, Mark 41
Emens, Jeff 50
English, G.H. 53
English, Kim 59
Entsminger, Guy 80
Eye, Morgan 11
Fairbanks, Douglas 9
Faurot, Don 17, 26, 27, 33, 37, 44, 48, 80
Fessler, Bill 48
Finley, Bob 77
Finner, Marlo 36
Fisher, Elvis 12
Fitzgerald, Mike 44

Flamank, George 84
Flores, Christine 67
Flynn, Laurie 86
Ford, Cornell 94
Frankenstein 39
Franklin, James 16, 39, 43, 57, 62, 91
Frazier, Lamont 36
Gabbert, Blaine 18, 38, 47, 73
Gibson, Bill 84
Gibson, Marquis 8
Glorioso, Johnny 80
Goestenkors, Gail 67
Gray, Mel 40
Grimm, Derek 36
Grow, Doug 40
Haas, Bob 58
Hainey, Jana 85
Haith, Frank 72
Handy, Marty 86
Harry, Jake 73
Henley, John 40, 93
Henry, Gwinn 9, 26, 84
Henry, Jim 86
Henson, Josh 2, 16, 39
Hill, Andy 51, 57, 87, 94
Hitchler, Conrad 46
Hoffman, Bob 47
Holovache, Blake 50
Howe, Gordie 88
Hunter, Jim 37
Hurley, Jack 48
Ice, Harry 44
Inskeep, Matt 52
Irwin, Bill 86
Ivey, Pat 43
Jackson, Jerrell 47
Jackson, Kenji 75
Jamieson, Tim 50
Janes, Ron 56, 92
Jeffries, Bob 44
Jenkins, Darold 44
Johnson, Greg 86
Johnson, Jim 83
Jones, Corby 8, 82
Jones, Curtis 82
Jones, Felix 6
Jones, Jamie 13
Jones, Gwen 82
Jones, Shakara 67
Jordan, Shug 50
Josey, Henry 24, 39, 57
Kadlec, John 42, 80, 83
Kamitsuka, Becky 86
Kekeris, Jim 33

TIGERS

Kelley, Thomas 88
Kelsey, John 74
Knight, Johnny 88
Kreklow, Molly 3
Kreklow, Susan 3
Kreklow, Wayne 3
Kuhlmann, Hank 27
L'Ange, Terry 7
LaRose, Danny 58, 89
Lawrence, Kendial 24, 62
Lawrence, Matt 59
Leon, T.J. 56
Lemmie, Cedric 86
Lewis, Leo 34
Link, Chuck 74
Lissner, Amy 86
Lombardi, Vince 89
Maclin, Jeremy 65, 94
Manley, W.G. 76
Manziel, Johnny 39
Maschoff, Paul 84
Matter, Dave 62
Mauk, Maty 16, 57
McArtor, Gene 50
McBride, Ron 93
McFadden, Darren 6
McGovern, Connor 91
McGuire, Rick 63
McLean, John F. 71
McMillan, Terry 40, 79, 93
McRae, Austin L. 1
Mehrer, Chuck 37
Mims, Lana 63
Mims, Madeline 63
Moe, Dave 51
Moe, T.J. 47, 51, 75
Moore, William 13
Morse, Mitch 91
Morton, Jack 33
Moseley, John 49, 74
Moss, Leroy 5
Musgrave, Bob 77
Musgraves, Dennis 7
Nebel, Art 66
Nelson, Jim 7
Nottelmann, Kristin 85
O'Brien, Dan 34, 70, 86
O'Dea, Pat 14
Olivo, Brock 51, 92
Onofrio, Al 5, 49, 74
Onofrio, Eddie 49
Otote, Jasmyn 67
Owens, Steve 61

Parseghian, Ara 5
Patterson, Frank 53
Patton, Chase 18
Peay, Francis 61
Perry, Jared 18
Peterson, Brian 14
Pfeiffer, Meghan 15
Pidcock, Dale 58
Pingeton, Robin 11, 67
Pinkel, Gary 2, 10, 12, 16,
    18, 23, 29, 35, 37, 38, 55, 57,
    62, 65, 68, 73, 75, 78, 94
Pinkel, Vicki 78
Pippen, Dan 90
Pisarkiewicz, Steve 34
Pitt, Brad 39
Plumb, Larry 37
Pobanz, Anne 86
Ponder, Randy 57
Poppe, Dennis 61, 79
Powers, Warren 37
Premo, Patrick 20
Reamon, Tommy 74
Reece, Bull 33
Ressel, Grant 64, 68, 73
Riccio, Sonny 10
Richardson, Steve 4
Ricker, A.J. 10
Robinson, H.O. 71
Robinson, Van 60
Rockne, Knute 61
Roper, Bill 76
Ross, Ricky 8
Rowe, Holly 28
Rowekamp, Bill 48
Ruby, Craig 20
Safford, Justin 59
Sakakeeny, Bryan 31
Sasser, Bud 57
Saunders, Tommy 29, 68, 87
Scardino, Tony 48
Schoonmaker, Bob 48
Sesay, Victor 10
Sharp, Rex 24
Shawhan, Tom 53
Shire, Sarah 25
Shuck, Glen 31
Sieck, Ron 7
Simmons, John 77
Simpson, Chauncey 33
Singleton, Ty 85
Sloan, Russ 27
Smith, Aldon 73

Smith, Bill 84
Smith, Brad 6, 10, 18, 35, 55,
    78
Smith, Brian 41
Smith, Clyde 26
Smith, Donnie 58
Smith, Justin 51
Smith, Larry 56
Smith, Ray 74
Smith, Reggie 36
Snowden, Phil 4, 27, 58
Snyder, Quin 72
Staggers, Jon 93
Steuber, Bob 44
Stevenson, Norris 30
Stewart, Norm 36, 72, 77
Stroud, Jack 7
Sutherland, Jason 36
Switzler, William 21
Taylor, Opie 73
Taylor, Ron 89
Taylor, Zaire 28
Temple, Tony 6
Thames, Kelly 36
Thomas, Chelsea 32, 85
Thompson, Burton 1
Thornton, Bree 15
Timmerman, Tom 38
Tobin, Bill 46
Tucker (no first name) 53
Valentino, Rudolph 9
Vann, Caitlyn 45
Ville, Zach 10
Wacker, Leslie 20
Wade, Maurice 44
Wagner, Crystal 15
Walker, Doak 80
Walljasper, Joe 16, 47, 73, 91
Wappel, Fred 4, 61
Ware, Bob 35
Washington, L'Damian 57
Weber, Keith 7
Wehrli, Roger 22, 79
Wendling, Steve 86
West, Devin 82
West, Mel 58
Wilkinson, Bud 93
Williams, George 20
Wilson, Andrew 43
Wolfert, Jeff 23, 29, 64, 65
Wynn, Lee Roy 77
Yost, David 18, 23, 64
Zastryzny, Rob 50

SCRIPTURES INDEX
(by DEVOTION DAY NUMBER)

Acts 9:1-22	78	Isaiah 8:11-9:7	49
Acts 16:22-34	73	Isaiah 53	19
Acts 19:11-20	8		
Acts 26:1-20	5	James 1:2-12	65
		James 1:19-27	87
2 Corinthians 1:16-20	30	James 5:7-12	3
2 Corinthians 5:11-21	43		
2 Corinthians 11:21b-29	56	Jeremiah 1:4-10	90
Daniel 3	46	John 1:43-51	39
		John 4:1-15	10
Ecclesiastes 4:9-12	42	John 6:53-66	29
		John 7:53-8:11	25
Ephesians 3:1-13	38	John 13:33-38	94
Ephesians 4:17-24	44	John 16:19-33	34
Exodus 3:13-20	69	Jonah 1	50
Exodus 14:26-31; 15:19-21	9		
Exodus 26:31-35; 30:1-10	64	Joshua 3	72
Galatians 3:10-14	58	1 Kings 10:1-10, 18-29	60
Genesis 1, 2:1-3	1	2 Kings 2:1-12	24
Genesis 18:20-33	27		
Genesis 21:1-7	61	Luke 3:1-22	82
Genesis 28:10-22	11	Luke 4:31-36	40
Genesis 39	16	Luke 5:27-32	26
		Luke 8:26-39	77
Habakkuk 1:2-11	21	Luke 10:1-3, 17-20	83
		Luke 13:31-35	41
Hebrews 3:7-19	32	Luke 15:1-10	28
Hebrews 12:14-17	54	Luke 15:11-32	53
		Luke 16:1-15	71
Isaiah 1:15-20	66	Luke 21:5-11, 25-28	17

TIGERS

Luke 23:26-43	67	1 Peter 1:17-25	74
Luke 24:1-12	37		
		2 Peter 1:3-11	59
Mark 3:31-35	45		
Mark 4:35-41	93	Philippians 1:3-14	13
Mark 6:1-6	62	Philippians 2:1-11	84
Mark 7:1-13	31		
Mark 8:31-38	79	Psalm 10	88
Mark 9:33-37	7	Psalm 30	4
Mark 14:43-50	68	Psalm 33:1-15	51
		Psalm 92	12
Matthew 3	91	Psalm 98	81
Matthew 4:12-25	20	Psalm 139:1-12	14
Matthew 5:43-48	89		
Matthew 9:9-13	23	Revelation 21:22-27; 22:1-6	70
Matthew 9:35-38	92		
Matthew 12:33-37	76	Romans 6:1-14	2
Matthew 13:10-17	15	Romans 11:25-36	63
Matthew 15:1-20	52	Romans 12:1-2	55
Matthew 16:13-17	85	Romans 12:9-21	35
Matthew 21:1-11	86		
Matthew 24:36-51	80	1 Samuel 3:1-18	36
Matthew 26:14-16; 27:1-10	22	1 Samuel 13:1-14	57
Matthew 28:1-10	75	1 Samuel 16:1-13	48
Nahum 1:1-8	6	1 Thessalonians 5:1-11	33
		1 Thessalonians 5:12-28	47
Numbers 13:25-14:4	18